the modern grandparent's handbook

the modern grandparent's handbook

The Ultimate Guide to the New Rules of Grandparenting

Dr. Georgia Witkin
Senior Editor, Grandparents.com

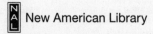 New American Library

NEW AMERICAN LIBRARY
Published by New American Library, a division of
Penguin Group (USA) Inc., 375 Hudson Street,
New York, New York 10014, USA
Penguin Group (Canada), 90 Eglinton Avenue East, Suite 700, Toronto,
Ontario M4P 2Y3, Canada (a division of Pearson Penguin Canada Inc.)
Penguin Books Ltd., 80 Strand, London WC2R 0RL, England
Penguin Ireland, 25 St. Stephen's Green, Dublin 2,
Ireland (a division of Penguin Books Ltd.)
Penguin Group (Australia), 250 Camberwell Road, Camberwell, Victoria 3124,
Australia (a division of Pearson Australia Group Pty. Ltd.)
Penguin Books India Pvt. Ltd., 11 Community Centre, Panchsheel Park,
New Delhi - 110 017, India
Penguin Group (NZ), 67 Apollo Drive, Rosedale, Auckland 0632,
New Zealand (a division of Pearson New Zealand Ltd.)
Penguin Books (South Africa) (Pty.) Ltd., 24 Sturdee Avenue,
Rosebank, Johannesburg 2196, South Africa

Penguin Books Ltd., Registered Offices:
80 Strand, London WC2R 0RL, England

First published by New American Library,
a division of Penguin Group (USA) Inc.

First Printing, January 2012
10   9   8   7   6   5   4   3   2   1

 REGISTERED TRADEMARK—MARCA REGISTRADA

LIBRARY OF CONGRESS CATALOGING-IN-PUBLICATION DATA:

Witkin, Georgia.
The modern grandparents's handbook: the ultimate guide to the new rules of grandparenting/Georgia
Witkin.
p.cm.
ISBN 978-0-451-23560-2
1. Grandparenting.   2. Grandparent and child.   I. Title.
HQ759.9.W58 2012
306.874'5—dc23   2011032114

Set in Garamond
Designed by Patrice Sheridan

Printed in the United States of America

To my grandparents, Ida and William, Sadie and Sam, for making me feel like the smartest and most talented grandchild in the world, and to my grandchildren, Jake, Ty and Nate—who really are.

And in loving memory of my mother, my daughter's grandmother, and my grandchildren's great-grandmother, Dr. Mildred Hope Fisher Witkin. You will read about her. Her élan lives on!

contents

the modern grandparent's handbook

introduction

A new grandparent is created every twenty seconds. . . .

And if you are one of them, welcome! There are a lot of us already—one-third of the U.S. population. There are now 70 million grandparents in the United States, and 1.7 million more every year. And while there are lots of books to help *parents* who worry about their baby's health, their baby's size compared to the charts, and what IQ-boosting toys they should buy for their toddlers, there are very few books for us. *Their* parents. The grandparents!

But do we really need a book about grandparenting? After all, weren't we parents already? Aren't we founts of help and advice? Thrilled and devoted? Ready to jump in and help, but wise enough to know when to bow out and be silent? The givers of gifts, and guardians of family history? Mature? Mellow? And marvelous?

Yes, but . . .

And isn't grandparenting natural? Weren't there grandparents long before there were books? Isn't it instinctive? Basic? And built-in?

Yes, but . . .

And haven't we grown up watching our own grandparents in action? We had grandparents, our children have grandparents, and now our grandchildren have grandparents. It's the way of the world, isn't it?

Yes, but . . .

You'll find that while your emotions may be universal and the problems are timeless, one thing is very different for today's grandparents. *We* are different!

Who We Really Are!

We are young.

Not just young in age, though we are. The average age of a first-time grandparent in the United States is only forty-eight years old. If you doubt it, do the math. If most mothers and fathers start their families in their twenties and their sons and daughters do also, most brand-new grandparents will be in their forties. And because we live so long now, we can expect to grandparent for at least half of our lives, and grandchildren can expect to enjoy three and four generations of family.

Not just young in appearance, though we are. When we were kids, grandparents looked old. They often had short gray hair, wore sensible shoes, sat a lot—and often ate soft food. Well, not anymore! Our hair is any color we want (usually blond), and as long as we want. Our shoes may be sensible by day, but look fabulous at night. We only sit still when we're doing yoga or at the movies or computer. And the soft food we eat—sushi and gelato.

But most important, young at heart—much younger in our lifestyles than most of our grandparents were at the same age. Let me give you some reasons why I say that. Grandparents.com recently commissioned a survey of today's grandparents, and here are our vital stats . . . :

We are dynamic.

We are dating and divorcing and remarrying, just like our grown children. My own three grandsons have eleven grandparents, thanks to their grandparents' divorces and remarriages! And by the way . . .

- Ten thousand of us say we were part of a demonstration last year or attended a rally.
- About seven thousand of us say we've gotten a tattoo.
- And, despite teens thinking that we have sex twice a year or not at all, according to studies, 38 percent of us say we have sex at least twice a week—which I think also counts as exercise.

We are financially powerful.

Thought we were retired? Think again. Most of us still have a full- or part-time job and we have money, honey!

- We control 75 percent of the wealth of this country.
- We spend $2 trillion every year on consumer goods and services.
- We have the highest average net worth of any other age group ($254,000).

We are generous.

Advertisers and fund-raisers go after the young consumers, but they should be pitching us!

- We make 45 percent of the nation's cash contributions to nonprofits.
- We spend $52 billion—with a b—on our grandkids alone.
- We spend, on education-related costs, $32 billion a year. Yes, with a b.
- And almost two-thirds of grandparents have provided financial support to their adult children and grandchildren in the last twelve months.

We are heads of households.

The stereotype of the grandparent living in the guest room is just that—a stereotype. Here's the reality:

- We head 37 percent of all households in this country— that's 44 million households nationwide, and the number is increasing at twice the national average.
- More than half of us no longer carry a mortgage. In this economy, that might explain why our children and grandchildren are moving back home to live with us. Six-point-two million households are now multigenerational, up from five million in 2000.

We are online!

An impressive 75 percent of us use the Internet, and nearly half of us not only follow grandchildren on Facebook, but we're also on other social networks, like LinkedIn, Twitter, and Yahoo! groups.

- 70 percent of us use search engines regularly.
- 63 percent of us shop online . . . at all hours, since the stores never close!
- More than four thousand of us have started our own blog.

And if you're like me, you have Skype to video-call the grandchildren (but hopefully have better luck finding a time when everyone can gather around to use it than I do!).

> I was on vacation in Las Vegas when I found out that I was a grandmother. I ran to my room, pulled out my laptop, and saw my newborn granddaughter—through Skype! After that, I went down to the casino and, no matter what happened, I couldn't lose.
>
> —S.T., New Jersey

We are having fun!

Not just with our grandchildren, either. We are living young and staying young on our own too.

- Almost one in every five of us dances regularly.

- Forty-two percent of us play sports or exercise, more than two thousand of us are still running marathons, and about fifteen hundred have gone skydiving!
- We spend $100 billion on entertainment and $77 billion on travel.

We love grandparenting.

Bottom line on why we love grandparenting? Sixty-four percent of us say it's an opportunity to do a better job than we did with our own children.

- Two-thirds travel with our grandkids.
- Eighty-one percent have the grandkids for part or all of our summer vacation.
- More than half of all of us play video games with our grandchildren. My two-year-old grandson asked me to put in my password so he can play Angry Birds on my iPad—and then beat me!

And although 60 percent of us live close to our grandchildren . . . 46 percent wish we could live even closer. The good news is that 70 percent of us get to see our grandkids at least once a week, even though that often takes effort on our part. . . .

Our daughter lives about two hours away or, as I like to say, far enough for me not to butt in all the time but, I hope, close enough to become truly part of our granddaughter's life. I've been waiting for grandmahood for a long time. I am *soooo* excited. My philosophy on grandmahood is to have fun, to experience wonder, to be silly, to not "parent" our granddaughter. I figure I've already parented four times . . . now I just want the "fun" part, and I *think* that's my place as Grandma. Now . . . I just have to convince our daughter of that!

—R.K., Indiana

So forget the stereotypes and caricatures; *we* are the grandparents now!

What We Want to Know

Since we are grandparents like no others, our questions are like no others. We want to know how to pick a name for ourselves. What's wrong with "Grandma" or "Grandpa"? Nothing, but it's often already taken, since our parents, and perhaps even their parents, are still alive. With so many grandparents, stepgrandparents, blended and melded grandparents, and great-grandparents in most families, we want also to know how to be the favorite—or at least, among the favorites. We want to know if it's normal to have "favorites," to feel bored at times or stressed when grandchildren visit. We want to know how to make grandchildren smile without spoiling, and help their parents provide for them financially in this bad economy without becoming a purse or a nurse. We want to know how to handle divorce without hurting the grandchildren (our divorce, their parents' divorce). We want to know what our daughters-in-law really think about us and how to develop a better relationship with them so we can get even closer to our grandchildren.

How do I know what grandparents what to know? Well, first because I'm a grandparent. Three times over. Next, because I'm a psychiatry professor at Mount Sinai School of Medicine in New York City and have reviewed grandparenting research and designed many multigenerational surveys. Also, because I've covered grandparenting topics and interviewed experts as a host and as the health-and-lifestyle contributor to CNBC, NBC, and FOX News for a total of eighteen years. I've also researched and authored more than ten books on family stress, including *The Female Stress Survival Guide*, *The Male Stress Survival Guide*, *KidStress*, and *Stress Relief for Disasters Great and Small*.

But mainly because grandparents have told me what they want to know! As the senior editor at Grandparents.com, my articles, videos, and tweets have reached at least a million grandparents, and I got huge feedback from those grandparents. Every topic in this book has come from their notes and messages. They wrote to tell me their stories, their advice, their warnings, and to ask questions—not only of me, but of other grandparents as well. Over one thousand Grandparent.com readers chat with one another regularly as members of my Dr. GG group. Many others participate in groups focused on distant grandparenting, daughter-in-law problems, grandfathering, financial concerns, and much more. Lots participate in the online surveys. Some just read offerings or contribute grandparent humor. Grandparents from every walk of life and from across this country have asked for this book and have made this book possible.

And I thank you all and hope you enjoy *your* book!

chapter 1

what's in a name?

When Juliet was hanging out on her balcony talking to the moon, she asked, What's in a name? implying that names aren't important. But they can be. Very important. Especially to new grandparents. After wondering what the baby's name will be, wondering about our own grandparent name usually comes next.

Names matter to us not only because they often say something about who we are, our heritage, and our background, but also because they say something about how our loved ones think of us. That's why parents agonize over what to name their babies and baby name books are so popular. Go to Amazon.com and type "baby names" into the search box for books. I got 17,604 results! Impressive? Just wait. Go to Google, and type "grandparent names," "grandparent pet names," or "grandparent nicknames" into the search box. I got 145,000 results!

"Granny" Is an Apple. Call Me "GG."

My grandchildren call me GG. Actually, a lot of people call me GG. My grandchildren's friends call me GG, their teachers call me GG, my daughter's friends call me GG, and everyone at Grandparents. com calls me GG. It's not only my name now; it's a noun: "This is my GG," say the boys. With 145,000 Google hits for "grandparent names," how did I become GG? Here's how.

My mother was alive and well when my first grandchild was born. She was playing golf, treating patients, traveling to Buenos Aires regularly, tap dancing for exercise, e-mailing, handling her own investments, helping all her grandchildren pay for college and graduate schools, and saying she led a marvelous and exciting life even though she survived five different cancers, one every ten years, starting when she was thirty-four years old and spanning the next fifty years. She was "Grandma." She earned that name. No one used it but her. I needed my own name. And not "Granny" or "Nanny." I needed a name that honored my mother by carrying on "Grandma." So I became "GG" . . . for "Grandma Georgia."

It is not vanity or denial or a fear of seeming old that is driving boomer grandparents to look for new and different names for ourselves as grandparents. Sometimes, as in my case, it's because the older generation is younger than they used to be, still here, and they've taken the basic traditional names. In other words, we're not the only ones living longer—so are our parents and, sometimes, *their* parents. We are the first generation for which this is true on any kind of a widespread basis, and it adds another twist to the task of picking our grandparent name. Besides, not only are many traditional names already taken, but different names belong to different generations. Today, no more blue-haired grandmothers means no more blue-haired names.

In my family, we have five generations alive currently. My grandmother is Mimier—a French Canadian twist on *grand-mère*—my mother is Mim, and I plan to go by Mimi to my newborn granddaughter, although I admit, I guess it depends on what the baby can say when she is able to talk!

—H.S., Montreal

How many of us now go beyond the old standards? A Grandparents.com poll found the answer is most!

A Grandparents.com poll asked:

Have you chosen a flashy new grandparent name?

Yes. Traditional names are too formal.	64%
I had to! Grandmother was already taken.	23%
Why reinvent the wheel? A name is a name.	13%

It makes sense that we want new and different names for yet two more reasons. First, because grandparenting today is new and different in so many ways. We're more actively involved in our grandkids' lives. We're not just hosting the occasional holiday meal—we're driving our grandkids to soccer practice and taking them on trips. We're e-mailing and Skyping. We're going on the amusement park rides with them, not just waving from the sidelines. And since there's a less formal grandparent role, we want less formal grandparent names to go with it.

When my first grandson arrived, I decided I wanted to be known as "Grand Dude." It's a little different and distinctive and it has a touch of silliness.

—H.C., Arizona

And last, but not least, we're the most multicultural generation ever, and many of us want to take grandparent names that reflect our cultures. We're calling ourselves everything from A to Z: the Aborigine "Garrimaay" to the Zulu "Ugogo."

So, take your time, scan all those names, create a few of your own, and try them on. In fact, try more than one on. Find one that feels right. Then see how your children react. They are your grandchild's parents and will have to use that grandparent name all their lives when referring to you, so most grandparents give their children veto power. But most important, see how your grandchild reacts. It will be months before he or she is talking, anyway, so you have time. Once your grandchild gets that grandparent name, it's usually a keeper.

But a word of warning to first-time grandparents: Despite all your planning and consulting and choosing and trying on names, if your beloved grandchild starts calling you their own collection of sounds—*that's* usually the keeper, whether *you* want it or not. And since you're likely to be a grandparent for half your life, I really hope you like it. And chances are, you will.

> I sometimes wonder if I'm the only Momo (rhymes with yo-yo) in
> the world. I doubt it. My grandson gave me the name and I had
> no choice. But the first time he uttered the word, I melted!
>
> —J.S., Louisiana

Another word of warning to first-time grandparents. Even if you escape a name made up of baby babble, you still might not have a chance to pick your own grandparent name. Your grandchildren often pick it for you by accident or circumstance. That's what happened to my grandchildren's other grandmother. Everyone was dancing together at a family wedding a few years ago, including then five-year-old Jake and three-year-old Ty, our grandsons. The band started playing "She's a Bad Mama Jama" and the boys went wild. They loved the music and sound of those words: "Mama Jama." The kids kept pointing at their other grandmother whenever the band sang out "Mama Jama" and screamed with laughter. Soon everyone else was laughing too, and to this day she's called "Mama Jama." And loves it.

A Grandparents.com poll asked:

Do you like your grandparent name?

Yes. My grandchild chose it.	44%
Yes. I chose it myself.	43%
Yes. Even though someone else chose it.	9%
Not really, but I'll live with it.	4%
Not at all.	1%

So give your grandparent name some thought. Consider your heritage, what you called your grandparents, and what's still available. My husband Mike's heritage is Greek and Syrian, and he called his grandfather Jiddo. Our grandchildren heard the word "Jiddo" just once, and Mike became "Jiddo," too. Ask your friends what they like to be called, ask your kids what they think . . . ask yourself what you would like to answer to. But don't get too attached to the grandparent name you choose, in case your grandchildren know better!

Have You Heard This One . . . ?

If you don't have a nickname yet, and really want one, here are a few grandparent names you can play with, change, present to your children, or offer your grandchild, who will probably change it by just trying to pronounce it!

	Grandmother Names	Grandfather Names
Traditional	Big Mama, Bubbie, Eema, Gada, Gamma, Ganni, GanGan, Gram, Gramma, Grammy, Gramommie, Grandgran, Grandma, Granmama, Mamaw, Mammy, Mams, MayMay, MeMa, MeMo, MiMi, Mimma, MoMa, MomMom, Mumsy, Nan, Nanna, Nanny, NeNe, NiNi, Nona, Nonni, Ona	Banpa, Bappa, Beebaw, Boompa, Boppa, Da, Drampa, Gampa, Gamps, Ganpa, Gram, Grampa, Gampy, Gramps, Grampy, Grandad, Grandaddy, Grandpappy, Granpop, Gumpa, Gwampa, Pa, Pampa, PaPa, Papps, Pappy, PawPaw, PeePaw, Pop, Poppa, PopPop, Poppy, Pops

	Grandmother Names	Grandfather Names
Trendy	Ama, Aimee, Babe, Bamba, Birdie, BonBon, CiCi, Coco, Dally, Dandy, Fancy, Foxy, GaGa, G-Dawg, GG, Ginja, G-mom, Geeda, GeeMa, Glamama, Glammy, Go-Go, Grandie, Granita, Gummy, Kitty, Lala, Layla, Leelo, Lela, Lola, MamaMia, Manni, MayMay, Meemer, Mia, Minny, Momette, Mombo, Mona, Nano, Nicey, OtherMother, Onie, Pebbles, Pippa, Salsa, Soosa Sugar, Tama, Tamsy, Uma, Vanna	Ace, Adda, Baba, Babar, Badda, BigBop, Bobaloo, Bop, Bubba, Buddy, Buster, Buzzy, Chief, Coach, Dabadoo, Dadoo, Dandy, Dappy, DeDad, Dexter, Dodie, Doozy, G-Daddy, G-Dog, G-Man, Grando, Graddy, Grandy, Grandude, Mellowman, Odie, Napa, Nemo, Panda, Papi, Papster, Peepers, Peppy, Pompa, Poppers, Poppo, Puggles, P-Pop, PopZ, Puppa, Rocky, Skipper, Slick, Umpa, Umps, Wampa
Playful	Bambi, Bamboo, Banana, BiggieMa, Booma, Bubbles, Bunny, Cha-cha, Chatty, Cookie, Dizzy,	Babaloo, Baboo, Bebop, Big Daddy, BiggieDad, BigD, Beau, Bobber, Champ, Checkers, Dabba, Dadsy, Derby, DooDad, Domino,

Continued . . .

	Grandmother Names	Grandfather Names
	Dodie, Gabby, Gadget, Gitchey, Grampoo, Happy, Honey, Hugme, Jamagramma, Lovey, Lula, MamaBear, Mamacita, Mambo, MaxiMa, Mayzie, Moogie, Mumpy, Nanoo, Nooni, Peaches, Pittypat, PomPom, Snuggy, Sunny, Sweetums, Tinkerbell, Tootsie, Twinkie, Twinkles	Doozy, Dozer, Faux Pa, Go-Pa, Granpup, Grantie, Grumpy, Grumpa, Hee-Haw, HoHo, Huggy, Hummer, Jeepers, Paddles, Peppers, Podge, Pogo, Sarge, Skipper, SloPa, Splash, Tank, TeePa, Tugh, UmPaPa

And now that you have a new name, let's talk about more new experiences—those that will be new for you, and those that are new for all modern grandparents.

chapter 2

the truth about . . .
grandchildren

Now that you've settled on a name, or been given one by your grandchild, you're ready for grandparenting. Or are you? It may be years, even decades, since you've cared for a baby, so how are you supposed to act with this new one? Is it bad to "goo-goo" and "ga-ga" too much? How about buying grandtwins the same gifts? Should you worry about spoiling an only grandchild or neglecting a middle grandchild? You ask some of your friends who are already grandparents, and everyone tells you something different. My advice . . . don't stress! You'll be great if you rely on your common sense and your sense of humor. You've already done the hard part—parenting. Now it's time for the fun part—grandparenting. Besides, a lot of "conventional wisdom" about grandchildren is not true! So, in the interest of reducing grandparenting stress, here we go—grandparenting experiences you don't have to worry about, you can just enjoy!

Baby Talk

If you find yourself baby-talking to your new grandchild, go ahead. That's right. "Goo-goo" and "ga-ga" all you want. Science finds it's as natural as a lullaby. Even though your children may worry that baby-talking will slow down your grandchild's language development, I have good news for all of us grandparents who find ourselves baby-talking anyway!

Actually, baby talk encourages early communication, because the sounds are easier for a baby to imitate. Just think of it as easy listening for infants. So if you're doing it, *don't stop*! It's instinctive, and if you think that it gets more smiles and babbling from your grandbabies than adult talk does, trust your gut. You're right.

Studies show that when adults are around infants, we naturally . . .

- raise our voice pitch
- smile a lot
- put "eee" sounds at the ends of words (like "fishy" or "doggy")
- exaggerate our sounds (like saying "You're such a biiiig boy.")
- shorten sentences to two or three words ("Say hi" or "Where's your ba-ba?" etc.)

Does baby talk slow up development?

Not only does baby talk not slow up development, researchers say we're always automatically one step ahead of a child's language development and "pull" them along. That means we're helping their language development by doing what comes naturally, not hurting it. For example, when your grandchild starts using two-word sentences, we go to three- and four-word sentences without even realizing it. When they catch up, we automatically graduate to full sentences. Soon we're proud of how grown-up they sound—and grandparents' baby talk helped!

Does adult talk boost children's development or intelligence?

By the way, if your children are *not* using baby talk with your grandchild, that's perfectly fine too. But contrary to "common wisdom" and ads from children's talking-toy companies, research finds grown-up words and grammar won't boost a baby's IQ or maturity. If you want to discuss the periodic table of the elements with your six-month-old granddaughter, that's great. But don't expect her to know the atomic weight of boron. In fact, one study compared one- and two-year-olds who watched one of the nationally advertised baby "brain-enhancing" DVDs for six weeks to a group who saw the tapes for the first time, and found that the six-week watchers didn't use more words from the program than the group seeing it for the first time!

So why are so many grandparents who talk grown-up style to their grandchildren impressed by their grandchild's booming vocabulary? Experts say there's a spike in word learning that *naturally occurs* between twelve and twenty-four months of age. By then, even baby-talking grandparents have moved on to adult talk and their grandchildren are sounding brilliant too.

The bottom line with baby talk is . . . if you do it, enjoy it. Just don't forget to drop it when you're finally out for dinner and you're talking to grown-ups!

Boosting Your Grandchild's IQ

Since most of us think our grandchildren are brilliant, one of the questions I'm asked most often at Grandparents.com is, "How do I encourage my grandchild's intelligence?" Besides, grandparents know their grandchildren's parents are often busy with more than one child, work, bills, PTA, coaching, and their own problems. So when they're alone with their grandchildren, they want to help their grandchild be ready for school and be successful in life. Grandparents tell me they play classical music in the car when their grandchild is on board, that they have the Discovery Channel on the TV when their grandchild is in the house, that they play word games, use flash cards, and do math puzzles instead of watching cartoons with their grandchildren.

Well, I have good news and bad news for you. First, the bad news: The majority of researchers find that it's *not* possible to speed up a child's IQ development beyond their capacity! For example, you've probably heard about the "Mozart effect," showing that playing classical music for a baby could improve spatial skills. Well, a Harvard study found that the effect lasted fifteen minutes and then faded away. So if you and your grandbaby like classical music—play it! But don't expect it to make your grandchild the next Albert Einstein. You can't push their pace beyond their natural progression.

Now, the good news: You don't have to! You just have to stimulate the natural process. So don't stress if Grandpa is watching cartoons on Saturday morning with your grandchildren—40 percent of weekend cartoon viewers are adult men watching with children, and most of them did well in school and earn a living!

And don't feel guilty if you are watching sometimes too. Here's all you really need to do to stimulate their natural intelligence:

- Fime—By the age of two months, most grandchildren will know our faces, and seeing us gives them a sense of well-being. What a thrill it is when they react to us with glee! But remember, the process is built into babies. It happens on its own. All the stimulation needed for development is already built into *normal* life. All our grandchild needs from us is lots of face time.

- Talk Time—Even though 80 percent of parents and grand-parents say they use flash cards, educational TV, and com-puter games to boost children's intelligence, experts say that talking and reading is all they really need to fully develop their talents. So talk, talk, talk, and then read to them at night. Easy enough.

  By the way, natural talking and interaction also teach your grandchild about cause and effect by the age of six months. For example, call Grandpa and he comes! Cause and effect. Say, "Sit," to the dog and he sits. Cause and effect. Push the button and the toy plays music. Cause and effect. Your grandchild really *is* brilliant!

- Playtime—Stimulating imagination and laughter is usually grandparents' special talent and task. Parents are on over-load, brothers and sisters are doing their own thing, babysit-ters are texting, and day-care workers are dealing with too many children. We are often the only ones in our grandchil-dren's life who can spend lots of time playing peekaboo and find-the-sock. Make-believe helps grandchildren practice scenarios that prepare them for real life. Peekaboo stimulates the memory, and find-the-sock practices classification.

So here's the bottom line: Have fun having fun. It's a very special gift that sometimes only grandparents have the time to give their grandchildren.

Only-child Grandchildren

Another question I am frequently asked at Grandparents.com is about only children. Even if their grandchild's parents are happy with just one child, grandparents worry about only children. Polls find that most grandparents say they want their only-child grandchild to have a sibling, because they think an only child may be socially disadvantaged and lonely. But is that really something to worry about? Take the Only-child Quiz and find out:

1. Only children are shyer than kids with siblings . . . true or false?

Most grandparents answer "true." They are wrong. They think that having a brother or sister prepares a child to defend herself, so she is more aggressive. But a study of two hundred children found that only children are actually better fighters—at least verbally— because they've had to learn to fight mostly with adults . . . their parents! They are also as social, achieving, and popular as other children, if not more so, and lag behind in only one way:

rough-and-tumble play. So go play outdoors with them, don't let them win all the time, prepare them for other children with some tag and gentle teasing, and don't worry—by fifth grade, they are as rough-and-tumbling as other children.

2. Only children are lonely . . . true or false?

Again, "common wisdom" says this is true. But the real answer is "false." Not to worry! Demographic studies show only children usually have *more* friends than children from larger families. One reason is because children from larger families don't *need* as many friends—they are surrounded by kids all the time and can use a break, instead. Another reason is because children from larger families have had to practice hiding, hoarding, and protecting their special possessions from siblings, so they don't share their things with friends as easily as only children do. And finally, because only children, like all children, seek what they need, and if they need a sibling relationship, they create it with a friend or friends. Often, one study noted, they'll develop a friendship that is not only close, but also lasts decades, like a sibling relationship.

3. Only children are more anxious and high-strung . . . true or false?

Here's great news for grandparents of only children: This statement is false, according to at least five studies I've seen. Research finds exactly the opposite: Only children are *less* likely than children in multisibling households to end up in therapy when they grow up, even when raised in a single-parent household. One explanation may be because only children get the undivided attention of their parents and grandparents, so their problems are dealt with rapidly! Another is that they often have high self-esteem because they are their parents' and grandparents' only superstar and never have to share the limelight. Yet another reason is that they have learned to handle problems (and people) maturely, since their role models are us, not other kids.

4. Only children become selfish . . . true or false?

Now, some more great news for worried grandparents. Contrary to popular belief, this too is fiction. Actually it's the kids who grow up in large families who become more selfish adults, according to a study of over one hundred "onlies," age eight to sixty-five— probably because children in large families have to fight for attention from an early age and keep fighting for attention for the rest of their lives.

So, unless you got the quiz perfectly right, check out these. . . .

---

tips for handling only grandchildren:

- Praise them for who they are, not what they accomplish.
- Give them an assignment to *fail* at something when they're with you . . . so they won't think the world ends if they are not perfect.
- Encourage them to share . . . they don't get much practice.
- Find other kids their age when they visit—not only grandparents like you. In other words, don't hog them!

Grandtwins!

Now, here's the other side of the coin. In addition to mail from grandparents worried about having only one grandchild, I also get lots of mail from grandparents who are worried about having two grandchildren—at the same time! Grandtwins! At least three of every one hundred grandparents have grandtwins already, and the number is growing every year. Why?

First, because the chance of having grandtwins increases as the age of their mother increases, and women today are having babies at a much later age than before. If your daughter or daughter-in-law is over forty-five when she gives birth, for example, there is a 33 percent chance that it will be a multiple birth . . . and more and more are. Second, because the chance of having twins is increased— 10 percent—if a woman uses the drug Clomid as part of fertility treatment—and more do! And finally, the chance of having twins is about 30 percent if ovum donation is used . . . and it's used by women over forty more and more.

If it happens to your child, you should know that there are lots of benefits for grandtwins. They have a built-in playmate, are usually close, and really love each other (though studies find they tend to act up when their parents or grandparents are around). There's also less sibling rivalry between twins when they visit with you—because no one came first, so there's no "boss." And they're more likely to share, because they've never experienced a non-shared world.

You may worry that when they visit you they will be double the trouble, but they are also more likely to be easygoing than singletons—probably because their parents and even we grandparents tend to be less perfectionistic with two. In fact, teachers say that twins are often chosen by other children as favorites to "sit with and play with." So be the calm voice in the twin storm, and remember these . . .

I had a daughter and then had twins—a boy and a girl. That was years ago. Now my adult twin daughter, June, and her husband have twin boys. I learned from my own twins, so I knew they often felt like a matched set—not like individuals. So for my grandboys, I made Gabe and Max each a bulletin board. Now when they come over, we take loads of pictures. I let them pick the photos we put on the bulletin boards. But believe you me, I don't delete those extras!

—G.S., Ohio

Now for the words of gentle warning: As exciting as grand-multiples may be for you, don't be surprised if it's less exciting for their parents. First, the stress of twins may increase any difficulties that exist between the parents . . . so you may be getting emergency "help" calls from your daughter or son. And there may be a sudden tightening of finances with more mouths to feed . . . so you may be getting emergency "help" calls from your daughter or son.

You get the idea!

So what to do? Take the long view. Twin shock wears off fast!

• **Give it time:** Help out, but don't take over, because the logistics will work themselves out on their own.

---

tips for handling grandtwins:

- Encourage routines— singletons get much more structure, and children need predictability. When they're visiting you or you're visiting them, provide order in their lives with a regular schedule of meals, naps, and bedtimes. It'll be good for the grandtwins and good for you.
- Make each feel special in his or her own way (particularly identical twins), not just as part of a "set," and you'll find that grandtwins are double the fun.

- **Practice patience:** Your child or child-in-law may be demanding with you because your double grand-infants are so demanding with *them*. Don't take it personally.
- **Keep your sense of humor:** Pretend that you're writing a sitcom about having twin grandchildren, look for lines and incidents to include, and then write them down and send them to Grandparents.com for sharing!
- **Help the twins' mother,** your daughter or daughter-in-law, by reminding her to parent herself as well as the babies by resting when the babies are resting . . . instead of catching up on busywork or housework.

some fun twin facts:

- Fraternal twins tend to run in families.
- Most identical twins happen by "chance" and can happen to anyone.
- The more pregnancies a woman has, the greater the chance of fraternal twins. By a fourth or fifth pregnancy, the chance of twins is four times higher than for a first pregnancy.
- Geographically, rates of fraternal twins are greater in the Northeast than in the South.
- In the United States, Massachusetts and Connecticut reported the highest proportion of twins, 25 percent higher than the national rate, while Nebraska and New Jersey had twice the national level of triplet and higher births. (Center for Disease control and prevention)
- The most fraternal twins are conceived in July, the fewest in January. (This may be due to the effect of the length of daylight on the ovulation hormone.)

And here's the advice that five different sets of grandparents who have grandtwins give: Offer to watch the babies! Give their parents a chance to get out and see a movie, have dinner (or sex) together, or just veg and they'll know you love them as much as your new grandchildren—plus you'll get some alone time with the babies. It's a win-win!

So now that we've talked about only grandchildren and more than one grandchild born at the same time, let's talk about another favorite grandparent topic—birth order. Is the middle child really so different from the oldest? Is the baby really getting it easier? Should you be worried? By now, you probably know my answer—be curious, be informed, but don't be worried! Your common sense and sense of humor are usually a better guide than "common wisdom" and "magazine psychobabble"—particularly when it comes to birth order.

Birth Order Differences

If you watch your grandchildren to see if their birth order makes a difference . . . you're not alone! Most grandparents say they *do*, and according to some researchers it *does*. See if you can predict what the social scientist would say about your oldest, middle, or youngest grandchild. . . .

1. Who is most likely to become president of the United States?
2. Who is most likely to wait in line and take their turn rather than pushing for special treatment?
3. Who is least likely to go into therapy?

The answers may surprise you. . . .

1. Who is most likely to become president of the United States?

The oldest. Fifty percent of American presidents were born first, as well as twenty-one of the first twenty-three astronauts. All that early adult attention from us and their parents supposedly gives them confidence and makes them used to praise—and they work hard for *more* praise all their lives.

2. Who is most likely to wait in line and take their turn rather than pushing for special treatment?

The youngest. Probably because they learned to wait their turn. The youngest grandchildren are also more likely to be risk takers than older siblings, maybe because their parents and grandparents were not hovering by the time they were born.

3. Who is least likely to go into therapy?

The middle child. I'm sure that one surprised you! Studies find that within multisibling households, it's the middle child who is usually very well-adjusted, with good people skills, because they have had to get along with both older and younger siblings and their siblings' friends. So don't worry about the middle child!

Ask your middle grandchild: "What's the best part of a sandwich?"
If they don't guess it themselves, tell them, "The middle!"

—J.G., NYC

Nature Versus Nurture

So, here's the question most grandparents ask me: When it comes to personality, is it nature or nurture? Most grandparents tell surveys they think it's nurture. Researchers agree with grandparents—it's the way we bring them up. So . . .

- Praise your firstborn grandchild for who they are—not what they accomplish.
- Really listen to the middle child when they ask you a question or tell you about their day in school, and don't set up their older sibling as a model.
- Spend time alone with the youngest, since they'll have the least amount of alone time with their parents.
- And . . . enjoy them all!

Now here's an area most grandparents say they know all about—sibling rivalry!

Sibling Rivalry

Most of us feel like experts when it comes to sibling rivalry—we lived through it ourselves, and then again raising our children, are still in the middle of it with our adult siblings, watch it at every family gathering, and see it between our grandchildren. But how should we handle it? Well, I've found that there is a lot less to be concerned about than I thought when it comes to sibling rivalry, and a lot less to "handle." Just take a look at these researchers' findings:

1. The amount of conflict between your grandchildren is not necessarily related to their affection for one another.

2. Disagreements between your grandchildren can actually help them practice conflict resolution skills.

3. Arguments are often a way to establish different identities between brothers and sisters. (That's why fights are most intense between siblings of the same sex and/or close in age.)

4. Sibling rivalry can be a way to test their parents' or grandparents' favoritism, by seeing whose side they take.

5. Sibling rivalry is usually worse when you are around and paying attention.

tips for helping firstborn grandchildren

- Don't set goals for them that are too high . . . they are usually trying too hard already.
- Help them take themselves less seriously—tell them about the funny things (not the amazing things) their parents did when they were young.
- Baby them a little—no one else will be doing it!

tips for helping middle-born grandchildren

- Make a big deal over their accomplishments.
- Don't compare them to their older siblings.
- Make sure their older siblings and cousins listen to their ideas.

tips for helping youngest grandchildren

- Don't let them break *all* the rules—just the normal grandparent spoiling.
- Give them responsibilities, not just privileges.
- Use their names—don't call them "baby."

If you knew all this already—then you *are* an expert in the field of sibling rivalry and you probably already know that most sibling rivalry starts when brothers and sisters are children, and competing for their parents' and their grandparents' attention. In fact, a survey of over one thousand children administered for my book *KidStress* found that children said they were more stressed and annoyed by their siblings' behavior than they were about dictatorial teachers, strict parents, or about disloyal and hurtful friends. And the problem won't magically disappear when our grandchildren get older. According to *Psychology Today*, one in every three adults reports that they *still* feel sibling rivalry—and the real number is probably higher, since so many of us do not like to admit to family problems even on anonymous surveys.

So what to do about sibling rivalry?

First, review the five points above and be assured that some sibling rivalry is common, even "normal." That being said, we can still make sure we're not stirring the pot!

Don't make overt comparisons between grandchildren. It's a lose-lose communication. Your grandchild feels second-best and usually takes your comments as a negative, not as encouragement. In fact, if your grandchild compares himself or herself to a sibling in a way that's self-deprecating, point out their uniqueness and special abilities.

Do accept their angry feelings toward one another, as long as they can control those feelings when they are with you and not act on them. Grandparents are, after all, the heads of the family. The parents of their parents. So let them know what the family attitude is toward fighting. "You can be upset, but you can't hit." Or, "You can be angry but still be brothers." Or when a child says, "I hate her," add the modifier, "Right now. But remember yesterday when she helped you with . . . ?"

Do try to let your grandchildren work out their tiffs on their own—as much as possible and only when there's no physical fighting. The best way I've found is to repeat everything they say to you about the other. That way, they know they've been heard, but they learn they won't be getting anything from you but boring repetition. For example, if one says, "He won't let me watch my program," just repeat, "He won't let you watch your program?" And when he follows up by saying, "It's not fair," repeat, "I hear you. You're saying it's not fair." I'm betting that they'll soon walk away and work it out.

Here's the good news: Eventually, your grandchildren will feel that their bonds are stronger than their rivalries. One reason is that, as siblings become older, they are happy to have someone with whom they can share memories, family, finances, problems, and celebrations. In fact, that same *Psychology Today* study finds that only 4 percent of siblings stay angry forever. So hang in there, help out, and try not to take it too seriously! The grandkids will get over it.

Now it's time to talk about their parents!

chapter 3

the truth about . . .
the parents

My friends and I ask one another all the time: "How are the kids doing?" If you are a grandparent like me, "the kids," of course, are now adults themselves, and you are comparing notes to see how they are doing as parents. Well, the data says they are doing just fine! And we grandparents can take a lot of the credit. I'm not kidding. We are not only more involved and active with our grandchildren than any other generation of grandparents, but we are also more emotionally and financially supportive of our adult children than any other generation of grandparents. We may be a generation older than our children and two generations older than our grandchildren, but studies find we are more connected, and there is less of a gap between generations, than ever before. And *nothing* brings a family together even more than the joy of grandchildren!

What Generation Gap?

We've been hearing about the "generation gap" for years. In fact, those of us who are boomers (born in the post–World War II baby boom) coined the phrase. But that was then, and this is now. And things have changed for the modern grandparent. I saw it first-hand.

My mother, Mildred, told everyone that she followed in *my* footsteps, instead of vice versa. I went to graduate school; then she did too (and so did *her* mother, my grandmother). I wrote my first book, *The Female Stress Syndrome*; she then wrote hers, *Single Again*. I got a doctorate; then she went for hers also. And got it! When she became a grandmother and then a great-grandmother, she asked me to show her how to e-mail with her granddaughter and take digital pictures of her first great-grandchild. She said she followed me right into the millennium—and she did. And she closed the large gap between her generation and mine with every step.

My daughter, Kimberly, and I, on the other hand, walk side by side. We live in pretty much the same world—as each other and as my grandchildren. We are both professionals and professors. She may text more than I do, but I have more apps on my iPhone. She may beat my grandsons at Wii races, but I can beat them at Angry Birds. We both drive the same SUVs, TiVo many of the same programs, and use a lot of the same slang when we talk about the grandchildren: "Really?" "No way!" and "Shame . . ." She feels comfortable calling me for advice about my grandsons' allowance, grades, and teachers, but she also feels free to call me on it if I'm too worried about their cold or virus. Is there a gap between us? Yes—but not very much. And we're not alone.

- A new survey by Nickelodeon and Harris Interactive interviewed one thousand grandparents, two thousand parents, and two thousand kids and found that the generation gap is pretty much a thing of the past.
- Even if parents and adult children have different parenting styles, research shows that when grandchildren come

into the family, most tend to get closer and appreciate one
another more.

- 87.4 percent of grandparents tell Grandparents.com that
they believe their adult children value their role as a
grandparent, and 68 percent of grandparents say they feel
closer to their own child or children once the grandkids
arrive!

I've seen the gap close more and more. I hope you are seeing it
too, in your own lives and experiences.

> I always felt close to my two daughters, but there were rough
> times when I was raising them as a single mom. Now that the
> girls have their own children, our relationships have changed
> for the better. They're both working mothers, so now they really
> understand how hard it was for me when I couldn't be class mom
> or go on every school trip. Now instead of tears, we share laughs
> over some of the things that happened in the past.
>
> —M.P., South Carolina

The best part of being a greater part of our adult children's
lives than ever before is that we are more a part of our grandchildren's lives than ever before too. In fact, a Grandparents.com
survey found that:

- 93 percent of grandparents think we play an important role
in our grandchildren's lives
- 87 percent believe that grandchildren value our role and
influence in their lives

- 99.5 percent hope to show their grandchildren the world.
- 66 percent have already traveled with them.

And as for the generation gap between grandparents and *grandchildren*—it is shrinking too. I grew up in the fifties and sixties. I loved all the music I could dance to, loved rock and roll and the Beatles in particular. I still do. Imagine my surprise when my grandchildren's Wii Rock Band and Guitar Hero featured both rock and roll and the Beatles. Imagine my grandchildren's surprise when I sang along without even reading the words at the top of the screen. While they strummed the guitar and beat the drums to keep up with the cyberband, I danced and sang my songs: "(Sittin' On) The Dock of the Bay" and "Lucy in the Sky with Diamonds." "How do you know our songs?" my grandchildren asked. "I'm all that," I said. "Yeah!" they agreed.

Why are these gaps shrinking? Give *yourself* credit not only for narrowing the gap between your adult children and you, but also for narrowing the gap between you and your grandchildren! It's disappearing because we're using every modern technology we can to keep in touch more, often throughout the day, by checking social media sites like Facebook and Twitter. We're texting and sending photos from our phones, so for those of us who don't live in the same town or even the same state anymore, we can almost reach out and touch our son or daughter or grandchildren by using webcams or Skype on our computers or mobile phones. We feel more connected to our adult children and grandchildren because we are—we know what's going on in their daily lives, no matter where we live.

I was afraid of technology and resisted getting a computer for years, but when I became a grandmother last year, my daughter Annie gave me no choice! Annie bought one and sent it to me. I live in Florida, while Annie and her family live in Michigan. "I'll be able to send you pictures of the baby as soon as I take them," Annie told me, "so learn how to use that computer!" And I did.

I can't believe that I can see the baby using the webcam. I just can't believe it. I'll be able to see him getting bigger and learning how to talk and walk. . . . What was I waiting for? Why didn't I learn all this sooner?

Now I check every day to see if Annie posted any new pictures of Ian on Facebook or e-mailed me some new shots. We try to have a video chat every weekend so I can see for myself all the changes in Ian. I was thrilled that during one of our Saturday sessions Ian showed off his first few words—they included "Na-na"—or a close approximation . . . Nannnn!

—A.R., Florida

Riding to the Rescue . . . or Not!

And here's some more good news about the generations. Our children seem to be doing a better job with our grandchildren than they themselves think. How do we know? Polls find that kids give their moms even higher grades for parenting than the moms give themselves. And so do we. Most of us approve of the way our children are parenting our grandkids—sometimes because their style is just like ours was, sometimes because it's better. But there will always be some times when we don't wholeheartedly approve, or approve but have suggestions anyway, and wonder how to handle it. After all, we want to make sure we don't create a gap where none now exists, but parent-child dynamics can make suggestions sound like orders, questions feel like criticism, and advice seem like interference. So before you ride to the rescue—or try to—here are a few dos and don'ts:

Do ask permission before offering advice.

As far as parenting goes, you learn on the job. So you have to give your kids a chance—even if they make a few mistakes.

Don't wait to be asked.

Offer to help out if it looks like your children could use it, but be clear that you won't be hurt if they say no, and be flexible on your timing and expectations.

Do keep your advice focused.

If your child or child-in-law has a parenting question, answer it. But don't also throw in career advice or ideas about how to decorate the house.

Don't do the parenting.

Try to support the parents in their decisions—even if you don't agree 100 percent. By showing the parents that you have confidence in their decisions, you will give them the confidence to ask your advice on future issues.

I thought I was offering good advice when my daughter Marissa said her baby, Ava, would soon be ready for solid foods. When I was at the grocery store, I picked up a box of white-rice cereal—the same brand I had given Marissa many years ago—and brought it to Marissa's house. Well . . . Marissa said she didn't want to start Ava on white-rice cereal because she read some doctors recommend brown-rice cereals instead, because they won't raise the blood sugar and insulin levels as much. I thought Marissa was overreacting, but I returned the white-rice cereal to the store, anyway. Whether it's true or not, it's not worth a disagreement!

—J.P., New York

The basic underlying principle is this: Our grandchildren are *their* children. We did our parenting and now it's *their* turn. If their style is different, it isn't necessarily wrong—just different. If you are really worried, follow the dos and don'ts above. But if your grandchildren are healthy and happy, just step back and enjoy. After all, we already did the work their parents are trying to do—now it's our time for the fun.

Finessing Feedback

Although "patience and tolerance" is usually a grandparent's best mantra, silence is not *always* golden, and biting your tongue is not *always* the best idea. Sometimes constructive feedback is appropriate, but before you talk to your child about your grandchildren, remember that it's easy for your child to slip back into old roles.

Most still desperately want positive reinforcement from us, so, as grandparents, our challenge is to offer our kids guidance that they can hear as constructive feedback rather than destructive interference. How can we deliver advice in a way that will not make us sound critical or make our children feel defensive? Here are some tips to help keep it positive:

- Start any suggestions with a positive statement. Commend them for what you see them doing well. Repeat that praise.
- Sound helpful, not hurtful. Don't say, "You're not controlling the kids." Try, "You might find it easier to control the kids if you . . ." Add in some useful tips.
- If they become upset, remind them you have their best interests—and the best interests of their children—at heart. Admit that you may not be right, but are only introducing a topic of discussion. Tell them you're on their team, in their corner, and on their side.
- Share stories of your own mistakes—and follow that up with the story of how you changed, learned, and grew as a parent.
- Try not to criticize when you're angry, only when you're calm.
- If you do feel you have to say something—save it for the privacy of home, not in public.
- And most important, don't confuse who your children are with what they *do*. Even if you think they are handling an issue badly, that doesn't make them bad parents. Let them know that you know that!

The best way our own adult children can learn from us is through modeling—just like our grandchildren do. So show your children good parenting with your own good grandparenting. And learn from them too. That's the fun of seeing that your adult children have a different style of parenting than you do. They are giving you "tips" every day by behaving in a new and different way.

Our Kids' Parenting Styles

Now, suppose your child's parenting style is not a problem for you—or for your grandchildren—but seems to be a problem for *them*. Suppose you suspect that your adult child is wearing herself or himself out, worrying too much, doing too much, or trying too hard. And suppose you think they are not even aware of it! Trust your gut—you're probably right. There are some styles that transcend our children's individual differences and are worth watching out for.

The Panicky Parent

Today's parents are smart. Sometimes they may even be too smart—too keenly attuned to every possible danger. It's no wonder that many are always on alert. News channels have to fill the TV screen with riveting news all day and all night, so parents hear about every abduction, accident, incidence of illness, school problem, schoolyard danger, and school bus disaster anywhere in the world! There are specials on children's behavior problems, learning problems, emotional problems, drug problems, medication interactions, allergies, eating disorders, and Internet perils. Talk shows discuss kids sexting, drinking, cyberbullying, and getting pregnant. The information is so abundant and immediate that our adult children are aware of everything that has ever happened to any child—and many are fearful that it could happen to theirs. They can soon become hovering "helicopter dads" and overprotective "smother mothers"—always ready to swoop in and rescue their children from every possible danger, whether it be a scraped knee or a hurt feeling.

A Grandparents.com poll asked:

Are you the parent of panicky parents?

Yes, and I wish they'd relax.	60%
No, they don't freak out about things.	22%
Yes, but they're right to worry.	12%
No, but they should worry more.	6%

As grandparents, we can help by giving our grandchildren's parents some perspective. We've been through it when they were young. They survived riding bikes and climbing trees, viruses and infections, bullying and dead fish. Tell them! Remind parents that safety products (like helmets and car seats) work, that toys are much safer now, and that medicines have childproof caps. Help your children be more realistic about their children by remembering their own childhood. Only you can do that. You were there then, and you are here now. Sometimes being a grandparent means parenting your grandchildren's parent all over again.

The Child-centered Parent

Many of today's parents are putting their children at the center of the family. This doesn't sound like a bad thing. After all, aren't your grandchildren the apple of your eye too? Putting the kids ahead of their own needs, ahead of their marriage, may seem child-friendly, but when it is extreme, it can lead to complications.

When a child is the absolute center of the family, she can grow up without boundaries. This can lead to demanding, entitled kids who become demanding, entitled adults. Some acting out might be all right for a child, but future bosses and spouses will probably not be so tolerant.

Furthermore, being the center of the family is too much pressure for a child. Kids cannot fulfill all their parents' emotional needs and it's not fair to expect them to. Children in this position often feel they need to parent their parents—and that's not their job.

Actually, it's *your* job. Be there for your children when they are parents. Remind them to take time for themselves and their spouses or partners. As I've said before, offer to babysit so they can have a date night or weekend getaway, and you'll get to spend extra time with your grandkids.

> I'm a widower and went to visit my daughter for the weekend and babysat for my grandkids while she and my son-in-law went to see a movie. On her way out the door, my daughter told the kids to listen to Grandpa and then gave me a kiss on the cheek and thanked me. Well, I winked and reminded her of the old saying, "When Mama ain't happy, ain't nobody happy!"
>
> —J.B., North Carolina

The Frustrated-athlete Parent

The tremendous popularity of professional sports, college sports, kids' leagues, and women's and girls' teams, plus the push for children to have more healthy exercise, all combine to encourage children to do their best at athletics. Great. But what about the grandchild who's not athletic? The kid who gets taunted as being "uncoordinated"? And what if the taunting is coming from one of the parents?

I raised my daughter in Westchester County, New York, and my grandsons are being raised in suburban Connecticut. Both are communities that focus on sports. I watched my daughter play soccer halfheartedly for years, and now watch my one of grandsons take semiserious tennis lessons, and his younger brother Ty play every sport he can sign up for—and excel at them all. At these games, I've seen the children who wish they weren't there and the parents who wish they could change them. I've also seen the grandparents watching games with sympathetic eyes, unsure about what to think, say, or do for their grandchildren.

The first step is to understand how some of our darling children turned into pushy parents. Parents who are overly involved in their children's sporting activities may be reliving their own childhood fantasies—may have been excellent young athletes but never went on to professional sports careers, or may have been the opposite—*poor* athletes who want their own children to do much better. Only you would know for sure. Only you can help them understand their own childhood and motivation, and, therefore, help your grandchildren. But if you think they will not respond well to such a discussion, there is still something you can do.

Help your children figure out why your grandchild might not be living up to their expectations. . . .

- Is your grandchild old enough or physically developed enough to play a certain sport? Tennis, for example, requires a level of wrist strength that may take some kids longer to develop than others.
- Is your grandchild big enough for a certain sport? He may be the right age, but his particular body may not be big enough for that sport. Football is a good example. Kids who are small for their age may end up spending a lot of time on the bench—which never feels good.
- Is your grandchild emotionally mature enough? She may not be able to concentrate enough to follow a coach's directions. She may take criticism too hard. Team sports require an understanding of cooperation, the tasks of a specific position on the field, the concept of letting one person be the star scorer and someone else being the key defender.

Once you help your child understand that it's not just lack of effort or competitiveness that's holding your grandchild back, your child will feel less like a "motivational failure," and probably ease up on your grandchild—and on himself!

If your grandchild is not a "natural" at sports but their parent tells you that they'd like him or her to play anyway, use your grandparenting finesse to find out if your grandchild really wants to play. Maybe she does. If so, don't stand in the way. Suggest individualized instruction, a private trainer or coach, if possible. Make it a birthday present, or do it yourself! Talk about the fun of the sport, or the exercise. Reframe it, as psychologists say, so that she's out there for the sheer enjoyment of it. And when your grandchild is with you, introduce him or her to noncompetitive sporting activities in which kids only compete against themselves—running, swimming, jumping rope, biking, hiking, and others. The bonus of noncompetitive sports is that you don't have to deliberately lose to make them feel better!

Now, if your grandchild just doesn't really care about sports but does really care about getting picked on for a lack of athletic prowess, and is losing sleep or appetite, or is visibly upset, give their parent a lot of support if he or she wants to let him drop out. They will often be getting arguments from the other set of grandparents, from teachers or coaches, from their friends, or even from their spouse, so they'll really need your backup! Tell your adult child that you trust their gut as you trusted your own when raising them. Agree that there are many other things to do besides competitive sports, and that their child (your grandchild) has the right to live his own life, not *relive* theirs.

The Distracted Parent

Every grandparent can see it. When parents are stressed, our grandchildren are stressed. It's like an epidemic that spreads from grown-ups to children. Not only because their parents don't have time to listen or play, but because our grandchildren don't get to see their parents relax! Since children learn by watching (not lectures), they are not learning stress management at home. They are learning to do what their parents do—distract themselves instead of relax themselves. When parents spend time at the computer, playing with apps, watching TV, so do their children. The problem is that quality interaction may happen only when the kids are with us, their grandparents! Here's how to help your distracted child and your grandchild at the same time.

1. More Face Time

When the family is at your house, ban TV, texting, or answering e-mail at dinner with their children or during "family time." Tell your child that you don't want to miss out on precious moments that can never be recaptured, and that you don't want your grandchild to think that they can distract themselves from the family, either. Without directly addressing their stressed behavior, you are giving them an island of peace when they are in your home, and giving them ideas about "family time" that they can take back to their own home.

And when your grandchildren are with you alone, give them as much face-to-face time as you can. Ask questions. Really listen to the answers. Researchers find that face-to-face time from grandparents is correlated with less anxiety among young children and less delinquency in teens.

2. Less Junk

Sometimes our children are so busy that they say yes to junk food without even realizing it or pass it out as a pacifier or reward. Or they are eating it themselves and have to share with our grandchildren. Actually, sometimes we grandparents do this too. Guilty!

But the Centers for Disease Control warns that child and adolescent obesity has more than tripled in the past thirty years, and our grandchildren are chugging down three times as much soda as our children did.

So help your child and your grandchild by fighting the urge to say yes to junk. I know that as grandparents we want every visit to be "the best," and so we treat our grandchildren to their favorites, and sometimes lunch at the fast-food restaurant is on the menu too. Think twice. Go just once in a while. At least you'll be saving your child from hearing your grandchildren say, "But Grandma lets us have candy!" Besides, the grandchildren probably know where you hide your stash of chocolate, anyway.

3. More Manners

Teaching children manners takes time, so manners are becoming scarcer as parents become more distracted and busy. We may understand and sympathize, but from the Grandparents.com survey, I know many grandparents are upset about watching some children run wild in supermarkets and talk back to their parents.

> I'm not Emily Post or anything, but I like when children have
> *reasonable* manners for their age. But what I see so often is kids
> paying no attention and zooming into people, not apologizing
> and then just zooming away.
>
> —A.L., New York

Because politeness, kindness, respect for others, generosity, and empathy will all help children in life, we want our grandchildren to develop these virtues sooner rather than later. But scolding their parents for not getting to it will only increase their stress and make matters worse! Instead, make manners a learning game. Quietly and gently do your part. But at what ages can we begin to help them learn? Here's what the experts have to say:

- Sometime between three and five years old most grandchildren can learn to say "please" and "thank you," introduce themselves, and lean over their plate when they eat so their clothes don't get ruined . . . and your tablecloth stays clean!
- Children between five and seven years old can learn to switch the fork to their right hand after cutting food, use polite phrases like, "Excuse me," and eat potato chips one at a time instead of by the fistful.
- And eight- to twelve-year-olds should be apologizing when they knock things over, holding the door for someone who needs help, and turning down the music volume when others want to talk.

For me as the mom, manners related to safety should be the number one focus for the grandparents—especially when they have the child and they're in charge of the child. How to get into a taxi, how to behave in a car, holding hands if they take them to the theater or a show. Probably safety is where the grandparents should zoom in the most.

—A.L., New York

Helping your grandchild learn manners is one area where grandparents rarely get flak. Most parents are thrilled if their child comes home more polite or neater. You've helped your grandchild and your child look good at the same time.

But what makes me think grandparents can be better at it than parents? Experts! Etiquette coaches (yes, there are etiquette coaches who get hired to teach children manners) say role-playing works because children need a rehearsal of the right manners when they do it wrong, and nagging is just not effective. And who has time for role-playing instead of nagging? Grandparents. So try a tea party for young girls, a mock visit to a dugout for young boys, or a pretend White House visit for older children. And be sure to give them praise when they get it right. And, grandparents, everyone will thank you: their parents, their other grandparents, and the grandparents in the supermarket.

To me, the moral of all these stories is that parenting our children doesn't stop when they become parents. In fact, when they are stressed and distracted, they need us more than ever. We know what worries them in general and how to reassure them and comfort them best. We know what they are going through as parents, because we've been there and done that—with them! And we know what we needed when we were harried parents, and what our parents might have done to help us. Now we can pass it on. After all, when we are parenting our adult children, we are grandparenting at our best too!

chapter 4

grandparent rivalry—and
how to win (secretly)

If you're like me, you love indulging your grandchildren, love surprising them, love giving them presents, and love seeing the smiles on their fabulous faces when you walk in the door. It's so much fun! And so, if you're like me, you secretly feel a bit competitive with the other set of grandparents and want to be the favorite . . . or at least among the favorites!

If you do, don't be surprised or embarrassed. It's natural, it's understandable, and it's common. Grandparents who live far away worry that grandparents who live closer will be preferred, and grandparents with less money worry that wealthier grandparents will gift their way to first place. And if there's only one grandchild, the stakes are even higher.

A Grandparents.com poll asked:

Do you have a grandparent rival?

Yes, I can't help it.	62%
No, we're fine.	38%

But, of course, being the favorite grandparent every minute of every day isn't always possible. First of all, no grandparent can always give their grandchildren everything they want and never say no. Grandparenting may be more fun than parenting, but it's not a free-for-all. As my own grandmother used to say when she had to say no to a grandchild, "Anybody can be your friend. My job is to be your grandmother."

Next, we can't possibly outdo all the other grandparents all the time—even if we really wanted to. But thank goodness we don't have to. Just like grandparents, grandchildren have plenty of love to go around. We can love all our grandchildren—and they can love all their grandparents! You may not be your grandchildren's only favorite, or favorite every day, but if you treat them with love and respect, you will always be a winner in the end. And so will they!

And finally, if you feel like you're losing the "favorite" race from time to time because you're the grandmother-in-law and your daughter-in-law prefers her own parents' brand of grandparenting to yours, you're probably right! A Grandparents.com poll found 57 percent of paternal grandmothers (that's the husband's mother) often feel left out. After all, your daughter-in-law's own mother is grandparenting just the way your daughter-in-law was parented. It's familiar to her—seems "right." And besides, you were the first woman in her husband's life, know him longer and better than she does, she's probably compared to you too often, and, if you have a daughter of your own, you may play favorites yourself without even realizing it.

So, being "the favorite" may be only a grandparent's fun fantasy, but there are lots of strategies that can help you make your dream of being "a favorite" come true.

The Art of Spoiling

It's only natural to want to spoil your grandchildren, and that's fine; that's part of the fun of being a grandparent, and you shouldn't deny yourself this pleasure. But here are a few things to keep in mind. . . .

The "Spoiling Paradox"

Here's what I call the "Spoiling Paradox": A recent AARP survey found that 80 percent of us say we worry that our grandchildren don't know the value of a dollar, yet the *same* percentage of us admit that we spoil the kids. Why? We enjoy it! We want to beat the other grandparents in the love lottery. We want them to know how much we love them. And the number one answer in the survey: "It makes me happy."

So don't stop the fun, but spoil them intermittently, not constantly, and your efforts will mean more. So will the value of a dollar. Let their chores, grades, or bedtime cooperation trigger the treats and they'll learn to earn. You'll still feel like a hero, but so will they.

The "You Let Them Get Away with Murder" Complaint

Most parents get a kick out of seeing us so eager to please their children. They know we want to be "favorites," loved and remembered. They know that we've already had to be the disciplinarians, homework monitors, and the bedtime patrol . . . with them! And now we want the fun of pampering our grandchildren and being the good guys.

But they also know that what happens at Grandma and Grandpa's can affect what happens at home. The kids want to stay up past their bedtime the way they did at Grandma's, eat in front of the TV like they did with Grandpa, and watch cartoons in bed while having popcorn for breakfast while their grandparents were sleeping. When they try to get the kids back to their normal routine, the kids melt down, and the question becomes whether two days of babysitting is worth the aftermath.

How can you have the pleasure of spoiling the kids—without the headaches and scoldings from your children?

First, steal a technique from family therapy called "joining the resistance": Don't debate their parents; agree with them. In fact, overstate their position and make it yours. For example, say, "I've been thinking about what you said about the kids not knowing the value of a dollar, and you're right. In fact, it's worse than you thought."

Then, make your case and let them know that you realize that they have the tough job of dealing with the children *daily*. In fact, ask them for help. Get their advice about how to unspoil the children when they are with you. As you talk, they may soften their stand.

And last but not least, remind them of this:

Children are smart, and they know very well the difference between parents and grandparents. They know we grandparents let them get away with more TV, snacks, and games before bedtime, and that time with Grandma and Grandpa is just a temporary break from vegetables and homework. If they don't adjust immediately when they get home, they're either *milking it or faking it*!

The Secrets of Favorite Grandparents

1. Don't buy love.

Reassure yourself that your grandkids will love you even without the nonstop presents—and then prove it. Set a one-month gift or candy moratorium, and just play with the kids when they come over, or read to them, or teach them something special, like a tap dance or an old school song, instead of taking them shopping. Let yourself see that you are valued and loved even if you don't dispense gifts.

2. Don't load them up with contraband!

Gifts of toys and candy are a problem in another way too. If we take our grandchildren to the candy store, and they stuff bags full of candies and carry them back home, we've put their parents in the position of saying yes to junk or no to the special treats. The kids should not bring home varieties of toys and candies that are not allowed in their house, because then you won't be given many chances to become a favorite!

How do you avoid the dilemma? Communication. Certainly, make sure you know your children's household rules for your grandchildren before you take the grandkids to the store, and ask them to clear major purchases (like a bike or a Wii). Also clear big offers like a road trip or an extended sleepover—before making any promises to the grandkids.

3. Do listen.

Ask questions about their likes and dislikes, their games and friends, real and imaginary, their TV programs, books, and their electronic games . . . and then really listen to their answers. Listen when they talk spontaneously, when they talk repetitively, when they talk endlessly. Listen when they are silly and serious. As I've said before, *their parents just can't listen to them on a daily basis the way you can when they are with you on a visit.* Be the grandparent who understands. The one who is patient. The grandparent who accepts what they say without a lot of lectures and criticism.

4. Do find similarities.

Become one of your grandchildren's soul mates and they will feel a bond that will never be broken. Start by going through "favorites" lists and compare notes. I call them the top-three lists. Try top-three favorite . . . vegetables, meats, fruit, candy, snacks, colors, activities, holidays—then do "bottom three"—you get the idea. Then go through secret wishes, hardest school subjects, least favorite chores, scariest movies, and so forth. Every time you find a match, make a big deal out of it. Shout, "Match!" Write it down but mainly remember it. When you talk to your grandchild, even by phone or e-mail, try to bring up one of those similarities. Like, "Our favorite holiday is only three weeks away," or, "I had to eat our least favorite vegetable today because it was in the salad already."

Successful Sleepovers

Overnight visits aren't just about the fun, food, games, and grandparent rivalries. A sleepover is a chance to forge an even stronger bond with our grandkids—to learn something new about them and teach them something new about us. The children take a step toward independence, plus . . . the parents get a night off!

Sleepover Tips

Good sleepovers don't happen by magic. Especially the first time. So don't take it personally if your grandchild has a meltdown or needs to call Mommy and Daddy. It's happened to the best of us. Still, there are a few secret strategies. . . .

Make it familiar.

Show your grandchild "his" or "her" room in advance—and use the room for naps and playtime before the actual sleepover. Fill the room with items that are familiar to him, like toys, stuffed animals, books, and blankets. Buy the same comforter set or mobile if you can find them. Familiar things make kids more comfortable and more relaxed.

Keep the routine.

Follow the same rituals and routines your grandkids follow in their own home. Especially before bedtime. Whether that means a bubble bath and a cuddle, reading two books, or making up a story together, they're much more likely to fall asleep and stay asleep if they're using the routine. And they'll be much more at ease with you, which will make you more at ease, which will make them more at ease. . . . You get the idea.

Make your home their home away from home.

If you have the space, set aside the basement, a room, or even a corner of the living room as your grandkids' very own space. Let them keep their toys and games there. You're not only telling them they're welcome—you're backing it up with actions. This keeps them wanting to come back again and again. And, after all, that's the plan!

Be prepared for some homesickness.

Kids can get homesick—even when they're with their grandparents, whom they love. Before the sleepover, check their parents' separation anxiety. As you know, children follow their parents' lead. If they're nervous about the separation, you can be sure your grandchild will be too. If your adult children are not really ready to let your grandchild come over for a sleepover yet, don't push it. Wait until they feel more comfortable with the concept.

If your grandchildren are already sleeping over at your house and they're missing home a little, it's fine to call their parents to have a little comforting chat and to say good night. You should also remind your grandchildren that they are going home, that their parents, their room, their toys, their pet iguana will all be right there waiting when they return. Repeat the phrase "when you go home" several times. Let them know their parents miss them and have plans for when they get home. This will give your grandchild a sense of security.

Bend bedtime rules at times.

Even if your grandchild has been in your house a million times, things look different at night. You might want to let her sleep with a night-light, or the door open, or even in a sleeping bag in your room. She might want you to crawl into her bed. That might not be how you planned it, but admit it, it sounds pretty nice. Remind her that this is a special Grandma or Grandpa treat, not something they can expect every night at home. And if it takes her a little longer to fall asleep, be prepared to read her that second . . . or third (short) bedtime story. Be ready to give him that extra snuggle. You're likely to find these unexpected extra moments together are some of the most wonderful of all.

Helping them get to sleep.

You're probably going to let them stay up a *little* past their bedtimes—that's what we do. But at some point, your grandchild is going to have to go to sleep. Keep in mind that you can lead a child to bed, but you can't make him sleep. And exhausting your grandchildren with roughhousing and letting them run around the house will not work. It will pump their bodies with so much energy-boosting adrenaline that they won't be able to get to sleep. It's better to gradually slow them down, to help reduce their heart rate.

- Spend some quiet time with two- to four-year-olds. Sit on the bed. Read to them. Sing to them. Tell them calm, dreamy, relaxing stories with images of billowy clouds—not scary tales of monsters and dragons. Rub their backs. Your soothing voice and the feel of your warmth may be just the relaxant they need to feel that they're not going to miss anything and that all is right in their world. Whisper, "Good night," and leave the room.

- Make sure they're not getting too much caffeine. Many kids are stopping at Starbucks after school. Even if they don't drink coffee, soda, hot chocolate, and iced tea often have enough caffeine to keep a young person's body stimulated for up to six hours. Caffeine cutoff needs to be in the early afternoon.

- If they say they're just not sleepy, give them an opportunity to "fool" you. Tell them if they want, they can sit up quietly and look at picture books and fool you into thinking they *are* asleep. Before long, they probably will be.

- For five- to eight-year-olds, you can begin to add some logical consequence to what happens when they don't go to sleep. I'm *not* suggesting you punish them! Don't even use the word. But you can explain to your grandchild that each minute she disturbs you after your agreed bedtime is one minute less of energy you'll both have for playtime or adventure time tomorrow, because you'll both be tired. Remind her about your terrific plans and that she won't want to miss a minute of that. Then stay firm and follow through.

- Rewards work too. If your grandchild cooperates voluntarily, offer him verbal praise, support, strokes—and set up a reward system, like a chart in his bedroom. Each night he goes to sleep on time, let him stick a star on the chart the next morning. A certain number of stars earns a reward. It gives them a sense of control over their impulses, a sense of accomplishment, and it works!

- Older kids understand the concept of negotiation. Give them options of bedtimes within a range that you set. They can pick their bedtime anytime between eight thirty and nine thirty, for example. If they start bartering for more time, make that contingent on giving up other things important to them.

Great Sleepover Activities

Wondering how to fill the hours between dinnertime and bedtime? Grandparents.com came up with some ideas that will get your grandkids moving, spark their imaginations, and make the evening so much fun, they'll want to come back next week.

- **Balloon volleyball!** Players bat a balloon back and forth, using any part of their bodies, keeping it from hitting the ground. To make it harder, add more balloons.
- **Indoor safari!** Hide stuffed animals around your house before the grandchildren get there; then have your junior explorers search for wild game.
- **Time machine!** Scan old family photos, like childhood pictures of your grandkids' parents, on your computer. Print them out and let the kids create funny captions or stories.
- **Karaoke!** To make it even more fun, you sing along to your grandkids' favorite songs and see if they can tackle tunes from your era.
- **Game night!** Not video games—that's old hat. Teach them classic games they don't know, like jacks, marbles, or pick-up sticks.
- **Gotta dance!** Teach the kids your favorite ballroom dance. Since *Dancing with the Stars,* it's cool again!
- **Hula-Hoop it up!** You try it too. The kids will love watching you give it a whirl.

- **Take it on the road!** Museums, aquariums, and zoos around the country are offering families the opportunity to sleep overnight among the dinosaurs, dolphins, and deer. Call and find out if your local institutions offer this option. And as always, clear it with the parents.

- **Say cheese!** Snap photos with a digital camera all evening. Print the pictures while the kids sleep, then have them assemble sleepover scrapbooks to take home in the morning. And don't forget to make one for yourself. It's sure to be one of your most treasured possessions!

Before the birth of my first grandchild, I made a nursery/playroom in my home, and it's still filled with diapers from the smallest to Pull-Ups. I also have a collection of books, including the favorites of all four grandchildren, from *Goodnight Moon* and *Pat the Bunny* to *A Wrinkle in Time* and *Harry Potter*. When I see after-Christmas sales, I stock up on puzzles, crafts, and videos for the grandchildren as they get older—not to give as gifts but to put in the nursery/playroom. Action-hero pj's and Hello Kitty nightgowns are there too. Now our grandchildren have slumber parties with Nanny and Papa very often and . . . it's a joy!

—S.S., New Mexico

Perfect Presents

Giving presents is one of the great joys of grandparenting. And the more grandparents there are in a family, the more we think about it, plan for it, shop for it. Let's be honest . . . we secretly hope we give better presents than anyone else. The good news is that presents don't have to be expensive to be big hits. But they do have to be thoughtful. Not thoughtful as in kind—although that's a given—but thoughtful as in full of thought. Here are some suggestions from experts and other grandparents for how to make every gift a triumph.

Make sure they're ready.

Choose toys that are developmentally appropriate for your grandchild. Your two-year-old grandson might love dinosaurs, but a two-foot-tall growling dinosaur robot with glow-in-the-dark eyes could scare him to pieces. Maybe a dinosaur puzzle would be better.

Who's the present for?

Just because you love ballerinas, or your daughter did when she was six, doesn't mean your Little League–loving granddaughter does. Take the time to think about the child as an individual. She's not just any six-year-old girl; she's *your* granddaughter.

They grow like weeds, so sizes change, and so do their tastes. Favorite colors, favorite sports, all change. If it's really too much to keep up with, take them shopping with you. That way you get to spend extra time with them *and* get them something they love. If you're too far away and that's just not practical, find out what stores they're particularly into, call up the store, and ask the owner to recommend something amazing.

Make it an event.

Buy tickets to a concert or Broadway-style show you can go to together. To build the excitement even more, add in a band T-shirt or the sound track to the show you'll see. It's not just a present; it's memories in the making. Or create your own event:

- Take a walking tour together.
- Watch a movie being shot.
- Take a local dinner cruise.
- Attend a class together—like a trapeze class or tap dancing class.
- Create your own golf or volleyball tournament.
- Get tickets for a minor-league game.
- Assemble a BirthDAY box.

A BirthDAY box lets your grandchild feel grown-up and in charge by creating their own day with you in honor of their birthday. Here's what it is and how it started.

When Jake was eight, I decided that instead of buying him a present, I'd give him a chance to design his own "day" to celebrate his birthday with me and Jiddo in New York City. So I found a large empty box, filled it with colorful paper confetti left over from a New Year's Eve party; added newspaper and magazine ads for Broadway shows and movies and sports games and museum exhibits he'd like; added menus from some theme restaurants; added a bag to be filled at his favorite candy bar, Dylan's; and finally, added some cash to be spent by *him* on the day of the event for extras. I then wrapped the box in gift paper, and put on a big bow and a note that read: *Build Your Own BirthDAY. Good for one year.* Well, he did! He picked out a movie (*Harry Potter*), lunch at Big Daddy's (great waffles), a visit to the Museum of Natural History to see dinosaurs, a stop at Dylan's, of course, then dinner at Jekyll and Hyde restaurant, and a sleepover. He collected his "day" about a month after his actual birthday, so the event didn't get lost in the general birthday commotion; he spent his extra cash on two small plastic dinosaurs for his two brothers; and he said it was the best day of his life! Although we know Jake is prone to exaggeration, and smart enough to say things to make his grandparents feel good and feel generous, we still loved hearing it and loved the day too. So BirthDAY boxes became a tradition.

By now, the BirthDAY box is a big deal. I now have three grandsons, and the older two are thinking of things for their BirthDAY box all year long. This year, both Jake and Ty collected their day this week!

Jake, now ten years old, told me months ago that he wanted more Harry Potter in his BirthDAY box—and he got it. I put in brochures from the Wizarding World of Harry Potter in Orlando, Florida, some PowerBars, some cash and sunglasses. I also put in alternatives, but who was I kidding? Last weekend Jake and I went to the Wizarding World of Harry Potter together. Just us. We visited Hogwarts castle; drank Butterbeer soda; ate jelly beans that tasted like dirt, earthworms, and ear wax from Honeydukes; got stuck ten feet in the air for five minutes when the castle ride ground to a halt (and when the lights came on, we got to see how all the machinery made the projections and ride work), and then, after much deliberation, Jake used his cash to buy a wand and two stuffed animals for his brothers. This time, even I said it was a perfect day.

Four days later, seven-year-old Ty cashed in his BirthDAY box selection: Grandpa, "Jiddo," took him to a double-header Mets baseball game! If you were watching the game on TV, you would have seen Ty catching two foul balls (with Jiddo's help) and a third ball tossed to him by a player on his way to the dugout. You also would have seen him eating Cracker Jacks, holding a huge sign, and giving the third ball to the little girl behind him who didn't catch any herself. He called me during the game to say it was the greatest BirthDAY ever.

Now, here's the best part of BirthDAY boxes . . . you don't have to think about how to top this year's adventure next year— the grandchildren *do*! And the choices don't have to be as elaborate as Jake's was this year, since the point of the box is just to offer adventures the grandchildren can have with *us*, rather than gifts we drop off and never see again. Last year the choices we offered were local and modest (Ty selected a minor-league Connecticut Tigers baseball game, and Jake chose a trip to the free Sony Wonder Technology Lab in NYC, with pizza and a sleepover for each), and they were fun too! So try a BirthDAY Box of your own. Put in selections that you are able and willing to do, and then let your grandchildren create their version of a perfect day with you in honor of their birthday.

It's an art.

Next time you give your grandchildren art supplies or a creative present, include some oversize, self-addressed, stamped envelopes so they can send you some of their creations. They'll feel special knowing you care about their creations. And you'll have the world's greatest refrigerator art.

Make it special.

In fact, make it yourself. If you sew or knit, your grandkids might love to wear Grandma-made hats, or dress their dolls in Nana-designed dresses. And all of us can make family history by writing down our stories. Go through your old photos, scan and print them, and include the names of everybody in them and how they relate to your grandchildren. Create a memory book and they'll treasure it for years to come. And even if they don't realize it now, when they grow up they'll understand how much effort you put into your presents to them.

But, as thoughtful and careful as we might be, not all our gifts are going to be grand slams. As excited as you are to see their face when they open your present, don't be upset if they don't jump for joy. Kids act in the moment.

If a young grandchild is sincerely disappointed by a present, just say, "I'm sorry you don't like it. We'll do better next time." And then try to put your disappointment aside so there's no friction about it.

On the other hand, if an older child is rude about a gift, it's okay to let them know they've hurt your feelings. Giving children honest feedback not only helps them reflect on their behavior, it also shows them you have a strong, honest, close relationship. And that's what we're all trying to build.

The most important thing about any present is that it shows

our grandchildren we love them and that we're thinking about them.

A Reminder . . .

Even though we all (secretly) want to be the favorite grandparents, the very-most-number-one-top-above-all-else important thing is to keep it about the kids, *not* make it about ourselves. So instead of allowing the differences between us and the "other" grandparents to be a source of conflict, try to make it a reason to rejoice. Celebrate your different cultures, different skills. Be thrilled that the other grandparents have something unique to offer and that they care enough to offer it.

Then slip your grandchildren an extra cookie. Just kidding.

grandmothers-in-law* . . .
and the three things
they should never say

*Mothers-in-law who are grandparents.

In the Bible, Ruth praises, respects, and loves her mother-in-law, Naomi. Although some of my friends, patients, and Grandparents.com readers say they think their daughters-in-law (DILs) feel the same way, most say they are not as lucky as Naomi. They describe their mother-in-law/daughter-in-law relationships as one of the most sensitive and complicated relationships they've ever had. But at the same time, they know—we all know—it's one of the most important relationships we'll ever have, because if we don't have a working relationship with our daughter-in-law, we won't have a relationship that works with our grandchildren!

So if you have an excellent relationship with your daughter-in-law—cherish it! And if you don't, there are things you can do to improve it, and we're going to talk about that.

But first, it's important to know what many daughters-in-law really think of us. So . . .

Grandparents.com offered daughters-in-law a chance to vent about us, the grandmothers-in-law. The answers were immediate, intense, and anxious—frequently saying, "Whatever you do, maintain my anonymity." Of course, not all of the comments apply to all of us. They might not apply to you at all. But it's good to get a window into what our DILs are thinking. If you're sure want to know, here's what they said. . . .

Grandparents.com asked daughters-in-law about us and some responses were:

- Parenting advice? Thanks, but no, thanks. We want to raise the kids our own way—mistakes and all.
- Passive-aggressive is still aggressive. That story about how your son loves your home-baked desserts that you tell just as I bring out the cake I bought at the bakery? Very subtle.
- Let's stop standing on ceremony. I know it bothered you that I didn't send you a thank-you note for the baby's birthday present, but I'm not a rude ingrate; I just think of you as family.
- Yes, I am good enough for him. It's sweet that you think your son is perfect, as long as you also understand that I'm perfect for him.
- Money can't buy you love. Please ask for some gift ideas and limits at birthdays and holidays.
- I know I'm not like you. But that doesn't mean I don't respect the heck out of you. Remember, I married your son knowing full well that "you marry the whole family."

It's not news that some grandmothers-in-law and their daughters-in-law don't get along, but the extent of some DILs' hostility to us *is* news. One survey by iVillage in 2010 found that 51 percent of DILs said they would rather clean the house than spend the day with their MIL; and 28 percent said they'd rather have a root canal! And a Cambridge University study of hundreds of families over a twenty-year period found that more than 60 percent of women said their relationship with their mother-in-law was stressful for them!

All this is not a great mystery. After all, their mother-in-law (that's you) . . .

- was the first woman in her husband's life
- knows him longer (and maybe better) than she does
- is used to taking care of him . . . and can do it very well
- will expect to share holidays and all special occasions with her and her children
- will have her own relationship with her children . . . the grandchildren
- will usually taker her son's side . . . even if she doesn't say so aloud

But we can minimize the issues. Somewhat. Sometimes.

Mother-in-law's Guide to Getting Along with Your DIL

Why bother? For your grandchildren! Why make the first move? For your grandchildren! Why let things pass? For your grandchildren! Let's start with four guidelines:

1. See what your daughter-in-law is like with other people, and don't expect her to be different with you.
2. Treat your daughter-in-law with the same patience and politeness you show your own daughter or your friends or even new acquaintances.

3. If things get really tough, pretend you're writing a movie and become an observer instead of participant. . . . It will help to give you psychological distance and enough emotional breathing room to feel in control of your emotions, and sometimes a laugh.

4. Keep your sense of humor.

Never, never, *never* . . . Did you hear me? Never! (Or hardly ever . . .)

Want to calm the stormy seas? Here are some tips for grandparents-in-law from therapists, counselors, clergy, and those grandparents-in-law who have come before you—to make it at least a little better. The three things you should *never* say to your daughter-in-law—particularly if she is the mother of your grandchildren!

Never say, "My son is right. . . ."

I know this is hard, but if they are fighting, let them work it out by themselves. Furthermore, don't ask your son to take sides or choose between you and your daughter-in-law. Not even in private. It's too risky, it will make things worse if he tells, and your grandchildren are at stake!

Never say, "I think you should . . ."

Or any variation on that theme, like "I always . . . ," "When I was raising your husband . . . ," or "It would be better if . . ." In other words, don't give advice unless you're asked or unless you ask first.

Even then, think twice. Even if you are right! (Of course, if you are a physician and your grandchildren's health is at issue, you get a pass. Otherwise, think twice.) I know that you hear her own mother giving advice, but when her own mother gives advice, your daughter-in-law is used to it. It's your advice that sounds like criticism. Enough said!

Never say, "I just assumed that . . ."

Double-check all assumptions. Neither you nor your DIL is a mind reader. And assumptions are just plain dangerous. Every assumption will feel like a criticism to her and she could hold it against you. Remember, your DIL is in control of those precious grandchildren, and more than anything, you need to get her on your side.

Grandparents.com asked:

Do you give your daughter-in-law advice?

I pick my spots to raise issues that matter to me.	40%
I speak up only if I think the kids' safety is involved.	37%
I speak up whenever needed—it's my family, after all.	14%
I keep my mouth shut.	8%

I have been a mother-in-law to two daughters-in-law for over a decade. And what have I learned? Wear beige and keep your mouth shut.

—C.D., New Jersey

Is There Anything We Should Say?

Tell her stories about your son that will amuse her and interest her—not stories that will make her feel that you think he's perfect.

—A.L., New York City

The shift from being the parent to becoming a grandparent—usually one of many—takes a major adjustment most of us never anticipate. It's so easy to offer advice based on our years of experience raising children. But don't. It's so easy to tell our adult children what they're missing. But don't. It's so easy to tell them what they're doing wrong. But don't.

What *can* we say? How about some positive reinforcement . . . ?

- "I respect how you're raising your kids." They may not do things the way you did, but it's a different world today. Find something positive to say that will ring true.
- "Please let me do the dishes!" Or the laundry . . . or make dinner. Be there to help.
- "Don't worry; you're wonderful parents." They're probably nervous about every decision they make, and those kind words can make them feel so great—and so warm toward you!

- "Your children are wonderful." All kids go through difficult stages. They did, and they turned out great.
- "I'm here if you need me." You know they're up on all the latest information about child safety, diet, and development. Just let them know that if they want your advice, they can ask for it and you'll be happy to share it.
- "All parents feel insecure sometimes." Parenting can be learned only on the job, and no matter how many books they read or experts they consult or even if they ask for advice from you, nobody knows their child as well as they do.

Grandparents.com asked:

Do sons keep grandparents in the loop about grandkids as much as daughters do?

No, sons never call.	81%
It's about the same.	13%
Yes, they're even better.	6%

The Real State of the Union—How We Feel About DILs!

Grandparents.com conducted a poll to find out whether many mothers-in-law feel the same way about DILs as many of them seem to feel about us. The answer: In general, we like them somewhat more than they like us, or at least we're more tolerant of their foibles. Consider:

- Nearly 60 percent of MILs said their relationship with their DIL was good or excellent; only 24 percent said it was difficult or "a lost cause."
- Thirty-two percent said their relationship with their DIL has improved over the years, although 19 percent said it's gotten worse.
- In sharp contrast to the DILs' responses, only 16 percent of MILs said they'd rather clean the basement or just read a book than spend a day with a daughter-in-law. Forty-six percent said there's nothing they'd rather do than hang out with their DILs, although another 38 percent—perhaps a more honest group—agreed, "There's nothing I'd rather do—as long as she brings the kids."
- Seventy-six percent of DILs said they wouldn't ask their MIL for parenting advice. But only 17 percent of MILs thought their DILs *should* ask for mothering advice, while 36 percent said their DILs would never ask anyway, and a more content 47 percent of you said their DILs don't need any parenting advice.
- Can we talk? Ninety-six percent of DILs said they would never talk with their MIL about their sex life—but 13 percent of MILs said their DILs have talked to them about the topic, and only 3 percent of you said they wished their DILs who *do* dish . . . would stop.
- When the poll asked whether they'd rather have one of several young celebrity wives as their DIL instead of the one

they have, 73 percent passed and said they'd stick with the one they have, while 17 percent said they'd take anyone else. About 3 percent said they'd be happier with either Elisabeth Hasselbeck or Chelsea Clinton. (Seventeen percent of DILs said they'd rather have Chelsea's mom, Hillary, as their MIL—a secretary of state? And they think *you're* tough?)

The bottom line? Most of us are happy with our DILs, or at least less likely to admit we're not. But there are still a lot of bad feelings out there: While almost 60 percent of us tell surveys that we believe our DILs love or respect us, 15 percent are sure our DILs hate or just ignore us.

And whether they do or not, don't take it personally—just recite this poem my grandmother taught me:

"Everything they say and do is information about them, not you."

But what if you *do* have something to say? Now, remember my advice about *not* giving advice freely. Trust me, think twice. But let's say you have a fantastic, incredible relationship with your DIL and your input is something vitally important having to do with the health of your grandchild and you are a physician and maybe also have a Nobel Prize in Medicine. Okay, but, even then, *don't say it through your son.* Raise the issue calmly, with both parents, and in person . . . so they can see the sincere and concerned, noncritical look on your face. And have a sincere and concerned, noncritical look on your face when you're saying it.

Grandparents.com asked:

Are you the mother of the father?

Yes, and I do often feel left out.	63%
Yes, but my daughter-in-law keeps me involved.	24%
No, but the other grandmother is an equal partner.	7%
No, and the other grandmother gets left out.	6%

Improving Your MIL-DIL Relationship

This is one of the toughest relationships in a family. But is this so surprising? Think back. Remember, you had a mother-in-law too. Maybe you still do. You've been there. And even if you adored each other, there were probably some rough spots and problem areas. Keep this in mind when you're dealing with your DIL: *Empathize!*

The truth of the matter is that she is the mother of your grandkids. And that means that she's the gatekeeper. She controls when and how often you see them, and that means that the MIL-DIL relationship is critical. So what do you do if it's not going so well?

- **Don't drop in unannounced.** Ever. Because whenever you drop in, it will always be the most inconvenient time possible—or at least your DIL may think it is. Call ahead, schedule a time to visit. Better yet, offer a time to babysit so your DIL can have a little time to herself. And phrase it that way. She deserves a little time off. After all, you were there once; you know how tough it is. Then you come off as understanding *and* you get time alone with the grandkids!

- **Follow her rules.** At least seem to, and try to, follow them as much as possible. If you want your DIL to trust you enough to leave you alone with the grandchildren, you have to make her feel that you do things the way she wants them done. If you don't, your DIL will almost certainly feel like you disagree with her rules—and, by extension, her. Of course, you're doing nothing of the kind. You're just giving the grandkids a few extra minutes of TV time. I know, you're not criticizing . . . but she's hearing criticism. So be sure to ask her about her preferences and rules. This will eliminate one of the biggest points of contention that DILs complain about, and over time, your DIL is likely to back off on some of these rules anyway—especially if she thinks you're on her side.

- **Give her the benefit of the doubt.** Just like you're not criticizing her, maybe she's not criticizing you either. You've heard the expression, "It's not what you say; it's what they hear." There's truth in that. And it goes both ways. So maybe, just maybe, she asked you to vacuum the house before she brought your granddaughter over *not* because she's criticizing your housekeeping, but because the pediatrician thinks your granddaughter may be allergic to cat dander. Maybe.

- **Compliment your DIL.** Not just to her—although that's great too—but also to your grandkids. Talk about her in ways that highlight her unique qualities and special talents. Say nice things to your son about your DIL. These nice comments are bound to get back to your DIL, and she will not only appreciate it, but she might even come up with a few nice things to say about you too.

- **Respect her relationship with her own mother.** Don't try to compete. You're not going to win. She's known her mother all her life. She knows what every look means. Even if her mom is criticizing her, she's used to it. It doesn't hurt as much. And since she learned whatever she knows about mothering from her own mom, it's no surprise that her own mom is going to be the one she turns to for advice. It's only natural, so accept it.

- **Always think of the children.** Model the values and behavior you want them to learn. You want them to learn trust, compassion, patience, respect, and understanding. Be that example. And if your DIL doesn't act that way herself? That's all the more reason you need to do it. The kids need to learn those important ideals somewhere, and that can be you. As they grow older, and start to understand the intricacies and difficulties of family relationships, they'll only value your relationship more.

Do not compete with your DIL. It's her time to shine!

—B.L., Hawaii

Should Mothers-in-law Be in the Delivery Room?

To my surprise, this question kept coming up again and again among participants of discussions on Grandparents.com. Many say that new moms bemoan the invasion of privacy, the uninvited presence of a mother-in-law ruining a special and intimate moment with their husband. Many feel bullied into letting a mother-in-law in, and then feel obligated to include their own mother in a suddenly quite crowded hospital room. They talk of husbands unable to talk their own mothers out of plans to invade what they see as an almost sacred space (at least until the next couple needs it . . .).

As for the mothers-in-law, some of us counter that this is, after all, the birth of our grandchild, and that we're entitled to be there when it happens. Those who speak more frankly might point out that our daughter-in-law's own mom, sisters, or best friends all stand poised to beat us into the delivery room to see the baby first, and what we really want is not to be left out.

What's the delivery room etiquette?

If your DIL is about to give birth, you haven't been invited in, and you're feeling an urge to barge in anyway because you just know you *should* be there, here's a quick piece of advice: Don't do it. No one will be in the right state of mind to have a real heart-to-heart with you in the bustle of the delivery room. Hurtful words might be thrown at you, and the resentment your son or daughter-in-law may feel from your intrusion will not quickly be erased.

But, if the due date is a while off, and you want to make your hope to be included known, ask your son how he and his wife want

Grandparents.com asked grandparents:

Should grandparents be welcomed into the delivery room to see their grandchildren born?

Maybe, but only if you are invited.	56%
No, the delivery room is for the mother and father only.	38%
Yes, it's a family affair.	6%

things to go. Let him know you'd like to be present, but reassure him that it's up to them. Giving him the chance to say clearly, "We would like to be alone in the delivery room," goes over better than waiting to find out that "she doesn't want you there." (Any daughters-in-law out there reading this, my tip for you is to make sure with your husband that decisions on who is allowed in the delivery room are always communicated as team decisions.)

If your own daughter is giving birth, and she tells you, in no uncertain terms, that you're not going to be in the room, you may be able to take it in stride. After all, you've seen her at her best, her worst, and everything in between, since the day she was born. But you don't know a daughter-in-law as well, and maybe, up to this point, your relationship has been free of stress. So if you broach the subject of being present at the moment of birth with her, and she shoots it down, try not to be resentful. Remember, this is a lady about to give birth—she may be a little on edge to begin with. And you'll be giving her a great compliment if you can accept her rejection as if it came from your own daughter.

And finally, once the issue's been settled, make a plan with your daughter-in-law for coming to help out in the hospital or when the family gets home (maybe if she just turned down your request to be in the delivery room, she'll try to make it up to you by welcoming you for an extended visit when the baby comes home).

Above all, keep in mind that even if it's your daughter-in-law's first child, she's probably eager to discover the dos and don'ts of parenting on her own. Although you may be poised to share your expertise, this may be a time to sit back and bask in the glow of a new arrival while providing his or her mom with respect, patience, and love. There will be plenty of time to dish out your opinions as the baby gets bigger! (To your friends, that is.)

Your Daughter-in-law's Mother

Now, let's say you weren't in the delivery room and your DIL's mother *was*. Or maybe neither of you was in the delivery room but she got the first phone call. Or maybe she got to hold the new grandbaby first. The delivery room is the first theater where the grandmother-in-law/daughter-in-law drama is acted out. And what if your role is not the way you want it to be written? What if your daughter-in-law's mother seems to have the bigger role? Your grandchild is just born and you are already worrying that as the grandchild grows older, your DIL's mother will get more access to the kids, or get the first option on babysitting or holiday times. You're human. You're a little jealous. But you may not be completely right!

Although you might be absolutely sure that your DIL is writing you out of the play, but expanding her own mother's role, research findings say it isn't necessarily so.

Myth: Maternal grandmothers have more access than we do.

Sometimes yes and sometimes no. It depends on a lot of factors. Geography, for one. If your family lives nearby, you're likely to see the grandkids more. Free time also factors in. If you're retired but your DIL's mother is working, you're likely to get more babysitting assignments. And then there's the nature of your DIL's relationship with her own family. If it's not that strong, don't be surprised if you're the one she comes to for advice.

Grandparents.com asked:

Do maternal grandmothers have it easier?

Sometimes. It depends on a lot of factors.	48%
Yes, it's no contest.	28%
No, we're all in the same boat.	15%
No, they have even more issues than mothers-in-law have.	10%

Myth: Maternal grandmothers don't feel left out.

Again, it depends. Becoming a parent can trigger old issues between your DIL and her mother. They may end up refighting battles left over from childhood. And even if your DIL gets along great with her mom, she may think her views on parenting are as outdated as yours. Or more! Polls find that today's moms tend to rely on advice from friends, books, or the Internet.

Myth: Maternal grandmothers don't have to walk on eggshells.

Not on your life! Every grandparent walks on eggshells at times! If you know of one who doesn't, write to me!

	MIL	Mom
Grandparents.com asked moms: What character from pop culture best describes your mother-in-law and your mom?		
June Cleaver, the traditional, proper and ladylike mother from *Leave It to Beaver*	16%	21%
Marie Barone, the intrusive and over-nurturing matriarch from *Everybody Loves Raymond*	16%	16%
Blanche Devereaux, the feisty and sexually progressive Southern belle from *The Golden Girls*	4%	4%
Clair Huxtable, the educated and career-minded mother from *The Cosby Show*	9%	13%
None of the choices above does her justice	55%	46%

You and Your Son-in-law (SIL)

Becoming a grandparent takes almost as much on-the-job training as becoming a parent. Becoming a mother-in-law . . . ? Even more. And becoming the MIL of an SIL is sometimes the hardest of all. Just think about all the jokes about men's MILs. The premise is usually that most mothers-in-law think their son-in-law is not good enough for their daughter (or daughter-in-law is not good enough for their son). Although the jokes are not PC (politically correct) and are often offensive, they do convey the stereotypical SIL-MIL relationship. . . .

- Behind every successful man stands a devoted wife and a surprised mother-in-law.
- Q: How many mothers-in-law does it take to screw in a light-bulb?
  A: None. She always gets the son-in-law to do it.
- My MIL and I were happy for twenty years. . . . Then we met each other.
- I haven't spoken to my MIL in eighteen months—I don't like to interrupt.

The jokes are the bad news; now here's some good news. A British wedding Web site did a survey and found that while 47 percent of SILs surveyed said they loathed their mother-in-law, 53 percent said they loved her. And another study recently found that although two-thirds of wives said their mothers-in-law caused them "long-term stress," only 15 percent of the husbands agreed.

But here are some dos and don'ts that can keep your relationship with your SIL smooth (or at least as smooth as possible):

Do: Welcome your son-in-law with open arms.

He's the man your daughter has chosen—respect that. Think of him as a valued addition to the family. Even if your daughter complains to you about him, *do not* make it worse or add your criticism. It'll only come back to haunt you when she's over it. Instead, tell her, "Talk to him about it, sweetie."

Do: Respect your daughter's boundaries.

Even if you've always had an idea of what you'd like your daughter's life to be, and who she should marry, keep it to yourself. Trust your daughter to make good decisions about her life. After all, she was trained by the best!

Don't: Try to change your SIL.

If she wants to do that, it's your daughter's job—and we all know you can't really change anybody anyway. Try to see your SIL's good qualities and don't focus on one or two little foibles.

Don't: Compete for your daughter's attention.

Your SIL's relationship with your daughter is based on romantic marital love. Yours is maternal. They are so different that there is no comparison and therefore no competition. Your daughter values both of you, so don't put her in the middle.

Do: Spend time with your SIL.

Try to find some alone time together—maybe a lunch during the week or possibly an evening when your daughter is out with her girlfriends. You'll really get to know each other and establish your own, independent relationship.

The number one thing to keep in mind, whether you're the mother of the son or the mother of the daughter, whether you're nearby or geographically far away, whether you're very involved or laissez-faire . . . *you love those grandkids.* And the best way to see them, to develop a relationship with them, and to have an important role in their lives is to have a great relationship with the parents.

So follow the rules as best you can, keep most criticism to yourself, keep your sense of humor, and give it time. Studies find that after ten years, most mothers-in-law are loved! Really. Loved!

having favorites—and
other guilt trips

There is a Welsh saying: "Perfect love does not come along until the first grandchild," and most grandparents say it's absolutely true. Unfortunately, the thing that comes along right behind it is . . . guilt. "I live too far from the grandchildren." "I live too close to the grandchildren." "I should have done this." "I shouldn't have done that." "I'm doing everything I did with my own kids." "I'm *not* doing everything I did with my own kids."

Right after feeling warm and flush with love, proud and excited about this great new life full of promise, right after feeling delighted and glowing and overcome with awe, we often feel a little guilt or anxiety creep in. That's because we're human. We're not perfect, yet we want to be—often even more so for our grandchildren than we did for our own children. But we can't be perfect—so don't even try. We do all kinds of imperfect and perfectly human things.

The number one thing to always keep in mind is that it's our turn to enjoy the fun; it's our turn to skip the midnight feedings and toilet training; and it's our turn to kiss and hug and laugh and leave. So if you sometimes feel guilty about certain aspects of grandparenting, don't give in and don't give up. You can counteract it. Here's what you need to know and how to use the information . . .

Guilty: You Play Favorites

A British study recently found that one in six mothers admit that they have a favorite child, and close to 60 percent of our grandparents say they have a favorite grandchild—although they'll never admit to it!

Sometimes the favorite is the very first grandchild, sometimes the only girl or the only boy. Sometimes the favorite is the one whose personality is most similar to the grandparent's. Sometimes the favorite is the one who's least similar to the grandparent.

Grandparents.com asked:

Do you have a grandchild who is just like you?

Yes, but with all my flaws as well.	63%
No, they're all different from me.	22%
Yes, and with all my best qualities.	15%

So don't feel guilty. Feeling like you have a favorite doesn't make you a bad grandparent—it makes you human. Besides, you may recognize that one is funnier, one is more athletic, one is more easygoing, and so forth, but—and this is critical—you have to let them know that you *love them all equally*. And that's the message for your children or grandchildren if they are accusing you of having a favorite . . . that they are *all favorites in different ways*! Let them know the ways in which each is special to you and you'll not only be reassuring them that they really are all favorites, but you're acknowledging that each is different and that you know them each very well. Grandchildren love to feel special, and making them feel special in *different* ways is better than pretending that they are all special in the same way. They are not. And they know it.

Many grandparents find their "favorite" changes over time as different grandchildren need them more. This can be explained by comparing the situation to a puppy needing more attention than older dogs need for a while, or new seedlings needing more protection than grown trees, etc. Grandchildren usually get it— sometimes sooner than their parents do. Particularly if you show the love. Differently, perhaps, but equally!

Tip-offs

Seemingly innocent actions may seem like you're playing favorites. Here are some situations to watch for:

- When fawning over a delightful baby, let the older kids share in the spotlight. Cuddly infants often get more attention than older grandchildren.
- Try not to shy away from difficult grandkids—they're the ones who may need you the most. Encourage positive behavioral changes instead.
- Stay away from stereotypes. Ask a grandson if he wants to bake brownies with you or a granddaughter if she wants to toss the football. They may surprise you.
- Give each grandchild the same number of gifts. Even little kids know how to count!

If you had more than one child or have more than one grand-child, you know very well that all kids are different. Some are huggy-kissy and some are a bit more standoffish. Some are sunny and others are shy. So, if your relationship with your grandchild isn't firing on all cylinders every minute, that's normal. And if another relationship is going great guns, don't feel guilty. Do something about it. Spend some one-on-one time with each grandchild, and when you're with each one, praise the one you're with. After all, each one has their own unique and delightful qualities that are worth praising.

Guilty: You Get Bored

Grandparents.com asked:

Are your grandchildren ever boring?

Sometimes, but I don't care.	42%
No, they're endlessly fascinating every second.	41%
Yes, but don't tell them I said so.	16%

You miss them like crazy when they're not around, but after a day together, you can't wait to check your e-mail or read the paper or talk to a grown-up. It doesn't mean we don't love them, but it's true. You can push a swing for only so long before it gets tedious. If you're totally honest, you'll have to admit this happens sometimes. After you've read the same story sixteen times in a row, it does tend to lose a little of the magic.

Be honest.

But don't feel guilty about it. Instead, try these tips:

- **Shake it up a bit.** Go to a different park—one without swings. Bring a kite. Buy a new book. Don't be surprised, however, if the little one still wants to hear the favorite story after.
- **Remember, it's your grandkids' job to slow you down.** To make you notice that the roots of the tree look like an octopus. To remind you that swinging really high can feel like flying. To introduce you to Angry Birds and take you through six levels on your iTouch. So take a deep breath and try to see these things through your grandkids' eyes. The e-mail's not really that important, is it?
- **Keep in mind how fast time zips by.** It wasn't so long ago you were pushing your own kids on the swing and reading them the same story over and over. Pretty soon, your precious grandchild will be packing up the car for college.

Now on the other hand, what if you're feeling that you love them *too* much?

Guilty: You Love Them Too Much

You think about your grandkids endlessly. You tell everybody you meet—including the supermarket cashier and the cabdriver—how cute it is when they suck spaghetti through their missing teeth. You

Grandparents.com asked:

Do you love your grandchildren too much?

No, that's impossible.	75%
Yes, I can't stop thinking about them.	25%

post pictures of them all over your house, your office, and your Facebook page. (Well, who doesn't do that?) You just can't spend *enough* time with them.

Are you abnormal? Is it unhealthy? Should you be worried?

Whatever "normal" is, nobody's it. What you're really doing is comparing yourself to somebody else—somebody who's supposedly doing it "right." And then you just feel bad about yourself. Stop it.

You love your grandkids. That's great! They're lucky to have someone so loving in their lives. And you're lucky to have people in your life that give you so much joy.

On the other hand, watch out for these pitfalls:

- Make sure you're not so focused on the time you *won't* get to spend with your grandkids that you don't enjoy the time you do.
- Don't rely on your grandkids to satisfy *all* your emotional needs. That's not the kids' job.
- Be careful not to alienate the parents. They may not love the idea of providing you with endless grandchild time at the expense of their own family time.

- Consider the feelings of your husband or partner. Does he feel like he's losing out on your companionship and love because so much of your energy is devoted to your grand-kids?

And if your focus is getting a little out of whack, follow these three rules.

1. Keep up with your friends, your interests and activities. Let your life be broad and expansive, not narrow and constrained.
2. Enjoy the time with your grandkids, *and* the time you spend with your other loved ones.
3. Remember that our hearts are stretchy—there's room in there for many people.

Guilty: You Don't Think You Live Close Enough

According to a survey conducted by AARP, 80 percent of grand-parents think it's important to live near their children and grand-children. So, does that mean that if your kids and grandkids live far away you should just up and move? And if you don't, does that make you a bad grandparent? Should you feel guilty?

No and no and no.

Some grandparents have to move to be close to their grandchil-dren, because they are needed by their adult child—to help with child care, special needs, divorce transitions, or financial emergencies. But most grandparents have a choice. They also have an established life where they live, with work, friends, and other children and grand-children nearby. Besides, it's often your children who have moved away from you, not the reverse. Having your grandchildren far away is hard, but giving up the life you know and love can be hard too.

If you are considering moving to be nearer to your grandchil-dren, consider these factors:

- Is your child or his/her spouse likely to be relocated for work? Could frequent moves be ahead?
- Would a move uproot you from your social network? Do you make new friends easily, and how much would you miss the support network you currently have? Will you really e-mail and Skype everyone?
- If you're still working, will you be able to find a job in the new location?
- If you're single, will you be able to pursue your interests and favorite activities in your new home? Will you be able to meet people and find companionship?
- Your adult children are going to have a life of their own. Will you feel resentful that you moved to be near them and then they don't include you in everything?

But what if you can't move or don't want to? Consider the upside of being a long-distance grandparent:

1. You won't feel guilty because you can't babysit at the last minute.
2. Your children can't blame you for hovering ... or not hovering enough.

3. The grandkids don't take you for granted. Your visits are always special.

4. The parents are so thrilled when you visit—because they get some time off—they give you alone time with the grandchildren.

5. You're insulated from the day-to-day stresses, disappointments, and details of the complicated, hectic world of parenting. And after all, you already went through it yourself.

Grandparents.com asked:

Are you a long-distance grandparent?

Yes, and there are pros and cons.	62%
Yes, and there are no silver linings.	18%
No, all the kids are, happily, nearby.	14%
No, but I see the benefits of being long-distance.	7%

And here's the good news—there's never been a better time to be a long-distance grandparent. Between e-mail, cell phones, Skype, Facebook, texting, and tweeting, staying in touch is not a problem. And airline travel is much cheaper and easier than ever before. Just try not to let too much time go by between visits. After all, you can't get a hug on Skype.

Guilty: You're Not Perfect

You know this, right? It's obvious. But you feel guilty about every little thing you do "wrong" anyway. Whether you're too strict or too lax, too overprotective or too lenient—you think you're the only one struggling out there. You're wrong—you are not alone! Just to prove it to you, here are . . .

Mistakes Even Good Grandparents Make:

- **Encouraging tantrums.** The first thing we do when our grandchildren melt down is to comfort them. Don't. Experts agree that when children have tantrums, trying to distract them, baby them, bribe them, or—worse—giving in to them sends the message that it's not only okay to lose control, it's a good idea. That won't go over too well in the office when they are adults. Instead, let them know you understand that they're upset and you'll be happy to talk to them when they calm down.
- **Agreeing to do too much.** If you're exhausted, you already have plans, or you just don't feel like it, it's okay to let the parents know that you'll have to pass on that last-minute babysitting assignment. You won't be any good to your grandkids unless you're 100 percent in the moment.
- **Getting frustrated.** Trying to teach a six-year-old to ride a bike is not always easy. And no matter how many times you say, "Just keep pedaling," that doesn't mean he will. But keep it loose; otherwise you'll ruin the moment and lose out on a potentially wonderful memory.

- **Falling for the hype.** If the guy at the toy store or the ad or the brochure says it's the toy with the most advanced electronics, the most profound educational benefits, and the biggest price tag, we fall right in line. Blocks and crayons really let your grandchildrens' imagination soar.
- **Breaking too many rules.** We spoil them—we do—and it's our prerogative to bend the rules a little. Just don't ignore the nonnegotiable rules set by the parents . . . and by good common sense.

We all make these mistakes and many others. But that does not mean we have to punish ourselves, or think that everyone else is grandparenting so much better. They're usually not! Some moments are memorable, some are forgettable, but we're all on this journey together.

To help you let go of the guilt, I'll let you in on the grandparenting secrets I share with my patients, but you get them for free:

10 Secrets to Guiltless Grandparenting

1. **Put yourself on your list of loved ones.** Even if you don't make yourself number one on your list, take care of yourself at least half as well as you take care of the grandchildren and everyone else and you'll be way ahead. Watch your sleep, nutrition, and exercise—and make sure you're having fun too.

2. **Practice saying no sometimes.** The grandkids actually appreciate the extra TV time, special snacks, and new toys more if we dole them out a little less often. And you'll see that they love you even when you're not a pushover.

3. **Play *with* the grandkids—don't just supervise.** Your grandchildren will never remember all the laundry you did for them while they sat in front of the TV—but they'll never forget the time you went down the slide with them. And neither will you.

4. **Don't try to keep the grandkids entertained every minute.** Downtime is an opportunity for imagination, so don't feel guilty if you take them with you to run errands or just leave them alone for a while to read and relax.

5. ***Under*schedule yourself.** We tend to forget to budget our time and energy and we can wear ourselves out. If an emergency or another essential task arises, cross something off your to-do list before you add the new item.

6. **Expect the best from life.** Anticipatory anxiety never helps us really be prepared for grandparenting's big and little problems—it just adds stress even before anything negative happens. Make positive prophecies instead—they are often self-fulfilling!

7. **Be your own best friend.** Be on your own side. Listen to yourself. Pat yourself on the back when you do well. Forgive yourself when you don't. You teach this to your kids and grandkids—now apply it to yourself.

8. **Don't wait for permission to take care of yourself.**
    You don't have to make yourself so exhausted with all
    your chores and responsibilities that your children and
    grandchildren have to beg you to rest. That sets a bad
    example. Show them that you value yourself and your
    time by putting your feet up or taking time off for a
    movie. And if you can't give yourself permission, then
    I do!

9. **Treat your family the way you treat your friends.** We
    know who our friends are and we know what they're like.
    We don't expect them to change overnight and we don't
    take everything they say or do personally. We ask them
    questions, listen to their answers, and give them the ben-
    efit of the doubt. Do the same with your family—you'll
    be a great role model for your grandkids.

10. **Break the guilt habit and stop should-ing your-
    self.** Replace thoughts of "this is who I should be" with
    thoughts of "this is who I am." Take the grandparenting
    journey with less stress and more fun. You don't expect
    your grandchildren to be perfect—why should you have
    to be?

These ten secrets are based on the same principles of self-
acceptance that most of you are trying to instill in your grandchildren. So if you really want them to value themselves, you have to
show them how—by valuing yourself.

And now some thoughts about Grandpa, and the special value
that grandparenting may have for him!

Grandpa's Second Chance

Grandparents.com asked:

Are you and your spouse grandparent partners?

Yes, we're working together and having a blast. 61%

We're getting there; it's a new dynamic.   28%

No, we need to have a talk.   11%

If you are a grandfather now, you may feel that when you were a dad you were preoccupied with supporting the family, and now that you have grandkids, you're going to make this your second chance. You may be thinking that you're going to do it right this time, you're going to put more emphasis on your family, you're going to get involved. But you don't know how. You might feel awkward or like a fifth wheel. Well, don't. If you have to change a diaper, it is not brain surgery. You'll master it. And if you're past the diaper phase, there's plenty of playing and teasing and joking and toy buying and moviegoing to be done. Just make sure you don't leave all the disciplining and rule enforcing—and the diaper changing—to Grandma. Be grandparent partners.

If you are a grandmother now, and feel that your husband is not as involved as you'd like him to be, you can help him ease into the role. Remember, fathers weren't that involved with the kids years ago, so he might not know what to do or how to do it. He might even feel out of place with the kids. You can help him use the skills he does have to make a concrete difference in the lives of your grandkids.

If he loves to cook, maybe he can prepare the family meals. Better yet, he can cook *with* the grandkids.

If he's mechanical, he can assemble the new toys or help your granddaughter put air in the tires of her bike.

If he's a writer, he can start a journal of family history or help your grandson with his book report.

And grandfathers can teach the grandchildren values and life lessons in ways that grandmothers might not be able to do as easily:

- If he takes them fishing, practicing catch-and-release teaches kids the sanctity of life, while cooking your catch illustrates the circle of life.
- If he shows them how to fix the car, then he's helping themdevelopself-sufficiency and independence.
- If he takes them camping or hiking, he's demonstrating appreciation and respect for nature, which

grandparents.com came up with these fun grandpa-grandkid activities:

1. Start a DIY project. Paint a room, work in the garden, have fun . . . and start on that "honey-do" list.
2. Visit a factory. Many local factories offer tours—as do train stations and shipyards.
3. Have a paper airplane contest. You might just set your grandchildren on the path to a career in aviation!
4. Go to a ball game. It doesn't have to cost an arm and a leg. Minor-league and local college games—even Little League games—offer all the fun without the high price.
5. Grill together. Get the kids involved by preparing the marinade or the condiments, and save your appetite, 'cause Grandpa's making his famous ribs!

can stimulate reflection and awe never found in front of a video game.

The main point is that we shouldn't underestimate the value that grandparenting has for grandfathers, or the value that grandfathers have for their grandchildren. And now for another topic of value— the value of a dollar.

chapter 7

grandmoney

Remember that recent AARP survey I mentioned that found that 80 percent of grandparents say we worry that our grandchildren don't know the value of a dollar? And then the same 80 percent answered the survey that we spoil our grandchildren. We know it's wrong but we do it anyway. Why? The number one reason according to the survey is . . . "It makes me happy."

Now, if it will make you happy for your grandchildren to actually know the value of a dollar, and you really want to get serious about teaching them, start young.

Grandparents.com asked:

What is the most you would spend on a single gift for your grandchildren?

$51 to $100	35%
$26 to $50	24%
$101 to $300	23%
More than $300	9%
$11 to $25	8%
Less than $10	1%

At around the age of five, kids begin to understand how money works. This is the time we can start teaching them to save for the future. Even if it's only a few coins from each week's allowance, they'll learn how it can add up and allow them to buy something they want. So, instead of shelling out for every gift and trinket they want, help them develop their own savers' mind-set. Buying something they want with money they've saved is not only fiscally responsible but also psychologically gratifying for them.

Teach Your Grandchildren to Save

Of course we enjoy giving our grandchildren gifts—even spoiling them—but we give them a greater gift when we teach them to understand and value money as a finite resource, and to manage it properly. Want to teach your grandkids to save? Try these tips:

1. **Help them establish a separate fund or account.** For little kids, this could be a piggy bank or a jar; for older kids it could be a traditional savings account or even a mutual fund account. But it should be something the grandkids can have access to and watch grow. It should be separate from the account to which you or your adult children contribute.

2. **Show them the money.** Kids will be happy to rake leaves, shovel snow, or put away groceries if they get paid for it. And by doing so, they learn the concept of working for money. Pay them in small bills they can hold and

touch, and suggest they save at least some of it in that account or piggy bank of theirs.

3. **Teach them to be smart shoppers.** If they've saved up for a big-ticket item, or a not-so-big-ticket item, or even if you're buying it for them—shop around, check prices online, and ask them to help you do so. Find the best price, get the best value, and teach them by doing so that saving money is worth that little bit of extra work.

What about paying the grandkids for getting good grades? According to Ralph Waldo Emerson, "The reward of a thing well done is to have done it." Well, he said that in the 1800s. Now some school systems are paying kids and their families for perfect attendance, good grades, or improved standardized-test scores. It's called "incentivizing" the kids, and if schools are doing it, is it any surprise grandparents are?

Grandparents.com asked:

Do you reward kids for good grades?

Yes, we give cash gifts for great report cards.	60%
Yes, we take them out but don't give money.	22%
No, they shouldn't need incentives to do well.	19%

Here's the problem with regularly rewarding children for performance: grades, homework, making their bed, or listening to you. When the rewards stop—so does the performance!

Real life gives you intermittent feedback, not steady rewards, and as I've said earlier, it's much more effective. Think about it. In real life, you might often act kindly, but only sometimes get a thank-you. You might always try your best at work, but only sometimes get a pat on the back. The lesson you learn with intermittent rewards is that the payoff always comes—eventually! That message can keep you going forever—sure that hard work and kindness will pay off—eventually. Let's be careful not to teach our grandchildren that they should expect a reward every time they do well. That kind of message doesn't keep them going beyond the last reward.

Even though some critics say there's little evidence that rewards for good grades lead to stronger student performance, others believe they are more effective than none at all, and that by working for rewards, grandchildren are at least learning skills and know what success feels like. So should you reward your grandchildren for doing well in school? You decide. Points and stars that can be collected toward a future reward work best, of course, because that's most like real life. But whatever you do, make sure to clear it with the parents.

Make sure, also, if you offer reinforcement for performance, to consider how each of your grandchildren operates in life. After all, each one is unique. Getting As may be a piece of cake for one grandchild who hardly has to do any work to achieve them, while another grandchild might put in hours of dedicated study and get only Cs. Set individual goals for each child that are realistic and attainable.

And remember too that there are more kinds of rewards than just money. Praise or fun activities together are also great ways to let your grandkids know you're proud of their achievements.

Teach Your Grandchildren
"It's Better to Give Than to Receive."

But just so you don't think we're too money-focused, keep this in mind: Aside from being generous with our kids and grandkids, we're also giving to charities. While we grandparents account for 42 percent of all consumer spending on gifts, we are responsible for a whopping 45 percent of the money given to nonprofits in this country. Sharing the wealth and giving to those less fortunate is something we believe in—and a value worth teaching to our grandkids.

How? Take these few easy steps:

- **Be a role model.** Tell your grandkids about the causes you support and why. Let them see you write the check or, better yet, take them with you the next time you volunteer at the hospital or the soup kitchen.
- **Give the kids a chance to help.** Contact your place of worship or local charity and ask if there are volunteer opportunities for kids. Nothing will touch their hearts more than being able to help in a real and meaningful way.
- **Give regularly.** Show your grandkids that giving is not an unusual thing by giving something—even something small—every month. When you sit down to pay your bills, write one more check to charity. And let your grandchildren know about it. Just like saving a little each month, giving a little each month really adds up to something wonderful.
- **Make it personal.** Every time you give a gift to your grandchild, for the holidays or a birthday, attach an extra card that

says that a donation was made in their name to a charity or a gift was given in their name to a needy child.

These steps not only help grandchildren appreciate what they have, but it lets them know that not everybody in the world is as lucky as they are. Or as lucky as we are. And we are lucky. We grandparents have the highest average net worth of any age group in the country. Well, we've worked hard. We've earned it. Now enjoy it!

Have you had dinner with some of your friends lately? Or checked in on some of the discussion groups on Grandparents. com? Then you know we're all talking about it: how much we are helping our kids help their kids—physically, emotionally, and especially *financially*.

And thanks to a lifetime of hard work, planning, and saving, we are in a position to help. It's a myth that as a group, grandparents have big money problems. Some do, of course, but as a group, we are healthier and more productive than our own parents were when they became grandparents, and many of us are still working and intend to keep working for a lot longer than our parents did.

We may be careful with money because so many of us are, or will be soon, on fixed incomes, but according to a Grandparents. com survey . . .

- We control 75 percent of the wealth in the United States
- We make 45 percent of the nation's cash contributions to nonprofit organizations
- We account for 42 percent of all consumer spending on gifts
- We spend $100 billion every year on entertainment

- We spend $77 billion each year on travel
- We spend $52 billion every year on our grandkids alone
- 62 percent of us provided financial support to our adult children and grandchildren in the past year for day care, housing, education, health care and day-to-day expenses.

We didn't expect to be so involved in the lives of our adult children, and it's not always easy; but it is a great opportunity to forge stronger bonds with the grandkids.

It's admirable to be concerned about the financial well-being of your kids and grandkids, but don't let generosity cause money problems for *you*.

Grandparents' Money Mistakes

Maybe grandfather Warren Buffett already knows everything there is to know about money. But the rest of us might make a blunder or two. Watch out for these common mistakes that experts say grandparents can make when dealing with money matters. . . .

- **Enabling the kids.** If you're able to buy your adult children a house or car, that's wonderful. But make sure they're at least *trying* to develop financial independence. You know you're enabling your kids when they start counting on a monthly check or when their response to your gifts goes from gratitude to expectation. To head this off, have periodic open discussions with your children about what they should and should not expect from you financially.

- **Leaving last wishes a mystery.** Even if you don't have a lot of money, it's important to let your kids know what you plan to do with your estate. When you tell your kids explicitly what you'd like them to do with your money, they're much more likely to follow your wishes. If you don't guide them—to save it for college or to get out of debt—they might do something else with it.

- **Putting the grandkids before retirement.** When you're looking at your finances, be sure you meet your own needs first. You're not going to do anyone any favors if you give generously to your grandchildren and then show up on your children's doorstep needing *their* help. Make a retirement plan with a financial expert before you commit to any significant financial gifts to your grandkids.

- **Not giving money to grandkids.** Right now, there are estate-planning tax benefits to giving annual gifts to your grandkids—if you can afford it. If you're afraid you might need the money someday, give the gift but ask that the money be placed in an account where your children can use the interest but not the principal. If you ever do need it, your kids can gift it back to you. Again, talk to a financial expert.

- **Not talking about your kids' money.** Do your kids have enough insurance? Are they saving for your grandchildren's education? For their own retirement? These are important questions that we're often embarrassed to discuss with our adult children. Don't be. Have the conversation and, if necessary, have it with a financial professional as well. The last thing you need is to have an emergency arise in the lives of your children and grandchildren—and then you'll have to step in and you hadn't planned for it.

When it comes to money—yours, your kids', and your grandkids'—it's important to talk openly and honestly. But we often avoid sensitive discussions, especially about finances. Some of us just don't talk about money—it's unseemly. Some of us worry that discussing these things could only add tension to already complicated relationships. But we can talk about money, if we do it with respect and sensitivity. So take some time to have a frank discussion with your adult kids about these concerns and then do everything you can to plan ahead.

Tough Economic Times

Given the ongoing economic slump, it's only natural for some of us to be having financial issues. Maybe it's not you; maybe it's your kids. It's often better to be open about everybody's financial situation than to agonize over it quietly or to keep it a secret until it becomes a crisis.

What you can do . . .

The best way to survive in tough economic times is to learn more about investing. Do you know about stocks, bonds, diversification, fees on financial products? If you're not financially literate, you tend not to make plans, and then you won't have enough money. Do you know, for example, about annuities that pay out equal amounts for the rest of your life? Do you know about other retirement plans? Talk to an investment professional about your options. Study up.

Are you already retired? If not, many experts say you should put off retirement until sixty-five or later. This could boost your retirement income from Social Security 20 to 30 percent. You'll still earn the same total sum, but your monthly payments will be higher if they're spread out over a shorter period of time. Same for your pension—if you get one. Talk to a financial adviser about retirement planning.

It may seem obvious but it can't be overstated: The less you spend, the longer your money will last. If you are worried, start cutting your expenses, whether you're working or already retired. Some expenses are likely to rise as we grow older, like health care, so try to offset those by making trims here and there. Maybe you no longer need that extra car or don't have to eat out as often. Make a list of how you spend your money and you're likely to see where you can save.

If you are already retired, consider working part-time. Not only will that extra source of income make you less dependent on your savings, but people who work part-time in retirement tend to stay mentally sharper!

Your Will

Estate specialists say it's generally best to divide your estate equally among your children. But if you don't, talk to your kids about it now. Let's say you have two kids—one wealthy and one who's less well-off. If you want to leave a greater share to the child who needs it more, it's a good idea to tell your other child that's what you're going to do and explain why.

What you can do . . .

The main reason many avoid writing wills is because it's a task that can be both morbid and boring. But it's important. You can write one online, you can write one with a lawyer, you can write one on the back of an envelope. But write one. If you don't, instead of *you* deciding who gets what, the government will.

Or worse, your heirs will fight about it in court. Avoid creating a family feud by bringing your loved ones into the conversation and put it in writing. Update the written document as needed and let your family know where to find it.

And don't forget you can give your money now, while you still have the opportunity to watch your grandchildren enjoy it. The law now allows you to give an annual gift of $12,000 per child—tax-free—to an unlimited number of recipients every year. This may change, of course, but in the

---

great jobs for grandparents

1. Start your own business. From eBay businesses to consulting firms to opening a franchise, grandparents are thriving by working for themselves.
2. Keep a secret. Retailers, hotels, even airlines hire "secret shoppers" to go undercover as customers and report back on the quality of service they receive.
3. The write stuff. Take a swing at freelance writing. You can do it from home on your own schedule and write about what you love.
4. What's in store? Get a job in retail and you not only get paid, you might get an employee discount. Or get this: CVS has an innovative program for snowbird workers—you work in the north during the summer, then in Florida or other warm locales in the winter. That's cool! And hot!
5. Follow your joy. If you love to ride your bike, how about leading bike tours? Love art? See if the local museum is looking for any help. Or . . . how about being a model for a live drawing class? Not all the models have to be nude, you know!

meantime, Uncle Sam says yes! Talk to a financial professional to figure out the best way to gift to your grandchildren.

Residential Care

We grandparents are living longer and healthier lives than ever
before, but that doesn't mean some of us won't need some help—
and how will we pay for it? Before it becomes an emergency, discuss care and residential options and the finances to pay for them.
If you wait too long, you could find yourself in a bind.

What you can do . . .

This doesn't mean only having "the dreaded nursing home talk."
It might mean you're thinking of moving out of your big house.
According to a survey, 40 percent of adults in their fifties and sixties are planning to downsize from their current homes—if they
haven't done so already. Maybe you're thinking of moving some-
place warmer or closer to your grandkids, and maybe you're excited
about it. But leaving your home can be a bittersweet experience.
Make it easier by following these tips:

- Start sorting now . . . even if you're not moving for a while. You'd
  be surprised how much you've accumulated over the years and
  how long it will take to go through it. And be ruthless. If it's
  not beautiful, valuable, if you don't use it and it doesn't have real
  sentimental value . . . *toss it*! Otherwise you'll have to pack it.
- Involve your family. Your son may want that papier-mâché
  sculpture he made in third grade that's been sitting in your

attic ever since. Your granddaughter might want her mom's high school English papers. Spread the joy. The more you give away, the less you have to move.

- Celebrate your home. Commemorate your life there with a scrapbook, a craft project like a quilt, or on a blog. You'll preserve all the wonderful memories . . . and it's portable.
- Embrace the change. Moving can be hard and even a little overwhelming. But visualize yourself emerging on the other side of the transition with a new sense of independence. You might find downsizing a liberating experience. Less maintenance work. Fewer rooms to clean. More time for fun!

Getting Paid for Child Care

We love watching our grandkids and taking care of them, but if you're the regular day-care provider and you're feeling a financial pinch, there's no reason why your children shouldn't pay you something for your time and work if they can. They'll be getting

---

Grandparents.com asked:

Have you moved since your grandchildren were born?

No, but we may move soon.	74%
Yes, but it was hard on the kids.	13%
Yes, and it worked out fine.	9%
No, we could never do that to the kids.	4%

the best kind of child care at a discount—and you'll be getting financial help, not a handout.

What you can do . . .

Grandparents.com found that 72 percent of us take care of our grandchildren regularly, and 13 percent are the primary caregivers. It's a lot of work. Like a job.

Grandparents.com asked:

Do you ever feel like the babysitter, not the grandparent?

Yes, all the time.	55%
It depends on how badly they need me.	23%
No, they never treat me like an employee.	22%

And if you can't afford to donate your time, understand that it's not uncommon to accept some compensation from your children. Call around and ask day-care centers how much they charge. Find out the going rate for babysitters. Then ask for less. Your children will appreciate the savings and you'll still feel like you're the grandparent, not the hired help. What could be better than for you to make a little money doing what you love? Last word: Communication is the key to making the arrangement work. Have the talk.

Getting Scammed

Did you know there's a scam that's actually called "the grandparent scam"? There are scam artists and identity thieves who target grandparents for sales pitches, investments, insurance policies all aimed at "taking care of the grandchildren." If you think you've been scammed, or worry that you might be, discuss it with your adult children. They're a great second opinion.

What you can do . . .

How bad is the problem? The FBI has documented over $30 million in losses to scams, but since most victims are too embarrassed or ashamed to file complaints, the problem is likely much worse than we know. The Federal Trade Commission estimates that consumers actually lose billions to cross-border financial crimes involving telemarketers identifying themselves as lawyers, customs officials, or lottery company representatives, and grandparents are targets because they are so motivated by wanting to help their children and grandchildren.

If you get letters, e-mails, or phone calls telling you you've won a lottery that you never entered, it's a scam.

If you are contacted by a Mr. Jones, Mr. Smith, or Mr. Peterson and he needs you to "cover the costs" of collecting your winnings, it's a scam.

If anyone asks you to wire them money to collect your windfall, it's a scam.

If anyone tells you that you've inherited money you were totally unaware of and wants you to forward money to cover "processing" or "retrieval costs," it's a scam.

If anyone tells you that you can receive much higher than bank or bond returns—guaranteed—by investing with them, it's a scam.

To be doubly sure, if you have doubts, double-check with your adult children, your friends, or a lawyer, and if it's a scam, report the suspicious communications to authorities.

Grandparents.com asked:

Have you been touched by a scam?

The scammers have tried but failed.	39%
Yes, we've been victimized.	30%
I don't think we've ever been contacted.	17%
No, but we know other people who have.	15%

Basic Money Tips

It's true: "Money can't buy you love." On the other hand, money can buy you and your children and your grandchildren peace of mind. So here are a few basic tips from the experts I worked with on CNBC and FOX News to keep in mind about your money:

- If you're retired, it's important to have cash available. Keep it liquid in a savings account or a CD. You won't make a great return, but it's safe.

- Don't take too much risk. As we get older, we don't have time to make up whatever we lose in risky investments. So play it a little safer now.
- Spend some money on yourself. What are you waiting for? Use a little to make yourself happy.
- Spend some money on your grandkids. If it gives you joy, why not? Just make sure you take care of yourself first so no else has to.

Here's the "bottom line"—as the money experts always say: Be smart about your finances, but be flexible enough to enjoy the fruits of your lifetime of labor as well. I used to say it this way on CNBC and FOX News: "Take care of your money so your money can take care of you." Actually, now it's more like, "Take care of your money so your money can take care of you . . . and your children . . . and their children." And statistics say that the majority of grandparents today can help financially, do help, and we are happy we can.

chapter 8

home alone . . .
with the grandkids

Since your first precious grandchild was born, you've been anxious to babysit. Or else you've been anxious *about* babysitting. You're thrilled to be asked to spend alone time with your grand-kids, but you're nervous that you'll do something wrong. Or, if you're like me, both! Not to worry; we can get it under control.

First, remember that you've been raising children since your own first child was born, maybe even longer if you took care of younger siblings. If you're thinking that child-care assumptions and procedures have changed a lot since you were raising your children, it's true. And it's not. Children are still children, and you know how to deal with them. The real problem is this: These are not *your* children. These are your children's children, and your adult children have their own ideas about how they want things done when it comes to their children and house rules, bed-time, food and snacks, TV watching and game playing, manners, movies, truthfulness, and even Santa or the tooth fairy. Let's go through them all.

But first things first. Be sure you're aware of any food restrictions or allergies, and make a copy of the front and back of your grandchild's insurance card. No one wants to think about it, but if anything happens, you need to be prepared. Ask their parents what medicines, like Tylenol, or vitamins you should stock.

Next—no matter how much you already know about children, try to find out the wishes of your grandchild's parents. Ask them about feeding time, snack rules, bedtime, pacifier use, TV time, or Internet use, and then repeat what they've said to let them know you've heard.

That said, don't make yourself crazy. If your children tell you to feed your grandkids while standing on one foot and whistling "Dixie," and you're not a great whistler, you can hum instead. In other words, being a little flexible is fine. Your grandchildren might respond very well to the way you do things—which might be a bit different from the way their parents do things. They may respond even better. But don't gloat, boast, teach, or preach. If their way works for them, and your way works for you, let it be.

And do babysit! Researchers from the Johns Hopkins Bloomberg School of Public Health published a paper in the November 2008 issue of *Pediatrics* indicating that having a grandmother watch a child is associated with a decreased risk of injury for the child. Other research finds that having a grandparent present also decreases the likelihood of delinquency, smoking, and truancy. We are a force for good. That's one reason I play drums with my grandson Jake, and basketball with my grandson Ty, and computer games with the baby, Nate. When grandparents are involved in a grandchild's life, the children are getting attention from more adults who are just fascinated by them and not distracted by work. And in my case, the drums and games are fun!

Babysitting means . . . long days. Short years!

—H.P., Connecticut

House Rules

Don't be surprised or insulted if your children leave you copious instructions or talk your ear off with dos and don'ts. Years ago, there was one expert—pediatrician Dr. Benjamin Spock. Now new parents have a million of them—TV doctors, radio doctors, Web sites, magazine columns, and books too. So be patient. Babies and kids haven't changed, but lots of advice certainly has—and will again, and again. We know that our grandchildren are much more resilient and flexible than their parents think, but if you want to babysit often, just go along to get along.

Grandparents.com asked:

Do your grandkids' parents leave you over-the-top instructions?

No, they wouldn't dare.	44%
Yes, and I go along with it; it's a small price to pay.	32%
Yes, and I ignore them.	16%
No, but I wish they would.	8%

Keep in mind also that there is more than one right way to take care of kids, and although your grown children's choices might be different from yours, they could very well be right for *their* kids. And we can even learn a thing or two.

The most important rule of all when babysitting is to be patient—with your grandkids, with their parents, and with yourself. The less anxious you are, the less anxious the kids will be, and that will lead to calmer and less anxious parents. Then everyone wins.

But how do you handle some of the issues that tend to come up when you're babysitting? Let's talk about some of the common ones. . . .

Eating . . . or How Long Can My Grandchildren Exist on Just Pizza?

The short answer is . . . long enough for you to send him back to his parents.

Have you seen your kids offer your grandchildren every possible food option available? How about spaghetti and meatballs for dinner? An egg? Yogurt? Macaroni and cheese? A hot dog? Toast with peanut butter? A spoonful of peanut butter, no toast? Leftover fish sticks? Great. I'll heat them up. No? Cold? With yogurt. Got it.

Did you think to yourself, "My kids ate what I gave them and they were happy," or, "Kitchens are not restaurants and there's no menu"? Did you think to yourself that your kids are raising ridiculously picky eaters but didn't say anything because you didn't want to get in trouble with the 'rents? Smart move. But when the grandkids are alone with us, we do have a little more wiggle room.

If this is an important issue for you, try saying, "Today, we're having chicken for dinner." If your grandchildren don't want it,

Grandparents.com asked:

Do you approve of your grandchildren's eating habits?

No, they're too picky and
the parents indulge it.   41%

No, they get way too much junk food.   37%

Yes, the kids eat balanced meals
and they don't complain.   17%

Well, the grandkids really aren't
any different from the way my kids were.   6%

that's okay. They can eat later. Try not chasing them around with food. If they're hungry, chicken will start to sound like a good choice.

On the other hand, if your grandchildren love pizza, will only eat pizza, and, if you're honest with yourself, you have to admit that you love it too . . . get a pizza. Pizza is not poison—it's cheese and tomatoes and flour, baked not fried, and if it takes some of the stress out of babysitting, if it gives you joy, give your grandchildren pizza. After all, eventually they're going to grow up and eat other foods. (Probably!)

Similarly, some kids eat too much junk food. Let's say your grandchildren think cookies are the base of the food pyramid and their parents missed the memo on childhood obesity. If you don't want them eating fast food or empty calories, serve them healthier choices when they're at your house. Just don't have cookies and other treats in the cabinets. If they're not available, your grandkids can't have them. And again, if they're hungry, whatever you're serving will seem like a good option.

That said, maybe you want to treat your grandkids. Maybe you like to bake and they love your special cupcakes. Wonderful! One cupcake will not ruin them for life, and they'll probably remember your cupcakes, *not* your carrots, fondly. As the old saying goes, "Everything in moderation."

The truth is, when you think back on it, don't you have to admit that you catered to your own children just a little? Maybe you served each item so that they never touched one another on the plate? And didn't you give them a cookie or two? So if you cater to the picky eaters a little and you give in to the sweet tooth of your grandkids a little, it's okay. In fact, if you spoil them with their favorite food and a couple of extra treats, it's fine too.

Because—and this is the best part—you get to give them back to their parents when your babysitting is over. You're not responsible for establishing their eating habits for life. We're a little like Las Vegas. What happens at Grandma's stays at Grandma's.

Playing Outside . . . or Is It Time to Go Inside Yet?

The grandkids love to play outside, and you love it because they're not just zoned out in front of the TV or video game. But, to be totally honest, playing outside can sometimes be a little . . . boring. It doesn't take long for your mind to wander. . . . "Where's the nearest bookstore? Did I call Emily back? I have to pay the gas bill."

We've already spoken about getting rid of the guilt over feeling bored. Now let's talk about getting rid of the boredom—for you and for your grandchildren. You want to enjoy your grandchildren and you want them to see you having fun and relaxing. You want them to see you laughing—not to see the back of your head as you're e-mailing, working, or reading the paper. You want them to learn how to create excitement—and you want them to learn it from you! So here are some antiboredom tips from my grandchildren's mother, my daughter Kimberly:

1. **Play something *you* like!** To avoid the zoning-out syndrome, stick to playing something you like. You can make any activity you like fun for kids. Just tailor it to their needs. For example, if you like to play golf, forget the playground and take your grandchild to a putting green or miniature golf. Teach them something new, like how to hold the golf club or how to swing straight or even how to hit far. Of course, you won't play as if your grandchild were not there—just have fun

2. **Make the activity child-size.** For example, child-size softball by skipping all the scoring rules if they are young and saying, "See if you can hit the ball ten times in a row." "See if you can hit the ball a little farther each time." "See how fast you can hit the ball." The game will become fun and familiar, and the rules can come later.

3. **Make each activity short.** Don't expect golf, softball, or anything else to hold young grandchildren's interest for very long. You're not going to get in nine holes or innings. It's better to have two or three things planned

and break up the day into activities. Kids like to know what they are doing, so preview. For example, tell them, "First we'll play games with golf clubs; then we'll have lunch, and then we'll go swimming." (But only if swimming is something else you like to do.) Then weave in some downtime! You need it, they need it, and they should be encouraged to learn how to amuse themselves.

4. **Have supplies close by.** Before you go outside, have the kids pick a snack and a drink and take them with you. That way you are not dealing with a thirsty, hungry child during your day out and not forced to buy whatever junk is around because you're all starving.

5. **Keep it going.** Once you have established your fun outside activity, such as golf, it will become "your thing" with them. Instead of your grandchild thinking that playing with Grandma and Grandpa means going to the backyard and being ignored while we catch up on chores, they will look forward to doing your special activity together. As they get older, they will learn more and more about something you like to do, and eventually you can *really* play together. Forget nine holes; you might actually make a full eighteen!

Scary Movies . . . or Tell Me When It's Over!

When weekend visits or vacation visits or even afternoon babysitting gigs roll around, it's often take-your-grandchildren-to-the-movies time. But did you know that most children's movies—even the animated ones!—have at least one "scary part"? And even though your grandchildren may beg to see those scary movies, that doesn't always mean it's a good idea! Although children's maturity levels develop at different rates, and some can handle animation but not real action scenes, and others can handle scary videos at home but not on a full screen in a dark theater, there are some general guidelines. Here's how you can tell if a movie is too scary for your grandchild.

1. **Very Young Children.** First, very young children, two- to four-year-olds, still have a natural fear of dark, sudden noises, unfamiliar faces . . . pretty much everything the scary part of movies are usually about. So they're too young to watch alone! Be there to fast-forward the DVDs at home or, in the movie theater, take a break for popcorn when they're frightened.

2. **K Through Second Grade.** Five-, six-, and seven-year-olds may sound braver, but they have wild imaginations, lots of nightmares, and are prone to exaggerate, so some movies may still be too scary for them. Make sure the younger ones are on your lap or next to you, just in case they get scared. And explain to the older ones how "movie tricks" are done. Or ask them how they think it's done. This gives them some emotional distance from the scary part and reminds them "a movie is only a movie."

3. **Eight- and Nine-year-olds.** Now, when a grandchild gets to be eight or nine years old, they're usually more afraid of being *teased* about being scared than of actually being scared, so they do begin to deal with the scariest

of movies. In fact, some experts say scary films give children practice separating fantasy from reality and gaining control over their fears! But again, each child is an individual, so . . . know your grandchild! And most important, don't let their older brothers or sisters tease them if they're scared! And, grandparents, don't let anyone tease *you* if you're scared, either. Studies say scary movies can increase our heart rate and our blood pressure, and trigger adult nightmares too. So if you get scared, grab your grandchild and hit the concession stand!

Responding to Rudeness . . . or He Said What?

You're taking your two grandchildren to the movies and suddenly you come face-to-face with rudeness. What do you do? Because your grandchildren are watching, and learning, stay in control.

If the ticket booth attendant is being rude, for example, ask for the person's name, and then use it. It makes you sound like a teacher or a school principal, so you gain some of that authority, and it makes the rude person worry about whom you might report them to—since they're no longer anonymous.

Acknowledge everything the attendant says with, "I hear you," or "I understand," but keep repeating what you want. It's better to sound like a broken record than to sound off. Above all, don't raise your voice. You'll lose control of the conversation, and then *you'll* be seen as rude, and your grandchildren will certainly try the same technique the next time they are frustrated, maybe with you.

If your calm conversation doesn't work, jump to the endgame and ask to speak to a manager, who is probably eager to keep things running smoothly and to look good to customers. Your grandchildren will learn that there's more than one way to solve a problem.

My daughter was recently asked, "What was the one life lesson you learned from your mother?" If I had any doubt about children and grandchildren learning by watching us, or any doubt that they really are watching us, the doubt was blown away by her answer. I expected her to say something about hard work paying off, or family love conquering all, or laughter as the best mental medicine, but she didn't. She didn't say anything that had come from my lips, or anything that I had deliberately lectured her about. What she said was something she had seen, not heard. She said, "What did I learn from my mother . . . ? That there's always a way."

Go know. I'm so glad!

Disappointing Gifts . . . or Say Thank You!

Let's say that while you're babysitting for your two grandkids, Aunt Susan drops by with some gifts for them. But instead of games, DVDs, books, or Harry Potter stuff . . . it's clothes. Matching plaid vests and some socks. It can be hard for kids to hide their disappointment, yet we want them to be polite, seem enthusiastic, and to thank their aunt. Our job is to teach them, by example or by instruction, to thank someone for a less than perfect gesture, *without lying*.

Here's the formula—it works for grown-ups too:

1. A simple start is to *name* the gift. "Oh, a vest!"
2. Then *describe* it: "A plaid vest!"
3. And finally, a *thank-you-for-thinking-of-us statement*: "Wow, you bought these for us? That's so nice of you," And, "Thank you!"

Now here's the best part: Through all that, *not one lie has been told*.

White Lies . . . or You Didn't Tell the Truth, Grandpa!

Lies are not always avoidable. Grandchildren hear a steady stream of white lies every day from their parents and grandparents. We tell about four white lies a day, say surveys, and that adds up to about eighty-eight thousand during our lifetime. So what do we do when the grandchildren are visiting? It's tricky: We want to teach the kids that honesty is the best policy, but also not to be brutally honest if it hurts people's feelings—and that's the main reason most people tell white lies.

"I didn't get your e-mail."

"That dress looks great on you."

"You are the smartest child I ever met."

"The turkey tastes great."

Do any of those sound familiar to you? Harmless white lies, but consider the fact that we are modeling behavior that our grandchildren will emulate. And we want them to be honest, right? So try not to tell even those little face-saving white lies in front of them if you don't have to.

For example, you're looking forward to spending some alone time with your grandkids over a weekend, and your wife's brother-in-law drops by to watch the game with you on TV. You forgot that you had plans with him. . . . Now what? You don't want to admit that you're so forgetful, but you don't want to miss a minute with the kids . . . and they are listening. Skip the white lie like, "Think I have the flu, man," and just say something truthful and simple like, "Sorry—we have to reschedule—my grandchildren are here today!" A great answer. A great role model.

Skip telling white lies to your grandchildren too. Don't tell them they're the greatest singer in the world, the best basketball player you ever saw, or a total genius—they know you're not being completely honest and it will make it hard for them to believe you next time, and hard for them to tell the truth! Instead, give them compliments they can believe: how much you enjoy their singing or how good their jump shot is or how impressed you are with their grades or vocabulary—they'll believe, because it's true.

Manners Matter . . . or Who Do Those Children Belong To?

Manners are something that often get overlooked by parents, and we talked about them briefly in chapter three, "The Truth About . . . the Parents." But our role is important too, because while we're babysitting, we can help our grandchildren develop the skills they will need to interact with people for the rest of their lives. But manners develop over time and with maturity, so at different ages you should have different expectations. Here's a review:

1. **Ages three to five.** Experts agree! Sometime between three and five years old most grandchildren should be learning to say "please" and "thank you," to introduce themselves when they are asked their name, and to eat neatly.

2. **Ages five to seven.** Children between five and seven years old should be learning to switch the fork to their right hand after cutting food, to ask to be excused rather than jumping up when they have finished eating, and to wait when someone is talking to others rather than interrupting.

3. **Ages eight to twelve.** Preteens usually know when situations require manners, and should be holding the door for someone who needs help, acting appropriately in public, and turning down the TV volume when others want to talk.

Now, if you want to improve your grandchildren's manners, remember what I said before: Role-playing works; nagging does not. Role-play good manners with your grandchildren. And model good manners yourself! By teaching manners to your grandchildren, not only will you be helping them get along in the world, you might just get a thank-you . . . from their parents!

Gaming . . . or Just One More Level, *Pleeeaaase!*

Not very long ago, grandparents wondered how much TV viewing was too much for the grandchildren when they visited. Now, with the explosion of video games, we have even more to worry about. Especially since they're playing not only on handheld units but also online and on our pads, pods, and phones.

Can game playing really become an addiction? Many researchers say yes. When kids play video games there is a release of dopamine in their brain—the same chemical triggered by addictive drugs—and the better they perform in the game, the greater the release of dopamine.

If you want to know when to worry, watch for:

- lost sleep
- problems at school
- and an obsession with scores and statistics

Of course, social scientists say some gaming is probably good for our grandchildren. It gives them something that stimulates competition, and improves hand-eye coordination as well as patience. On the other hand, when they're playing these games they're reactive . . . pushing buttons . . . not reading. This is why child development experts say about thirty minutes to one hour a day is the maximum amount of time that should be spent on video games . . . maybe a little more time when they're visiting with you.

On a long airplane trip or when they're riding in the car for
a while, it's a great way for them to occupy themselves. And
honestly, it gives me a little peace and quiet for a change!

—L.N., Maine

Neuroscientists find children who spend more than thirty
minutes to an hour a day playing these games may be interfering
with some other areas of brain development, and children with
social anxiety who spend time alone never learn how to make real
friends. So if they're playing too long, don't be afraid to say no.

Grandparents can do anything. . . . They listen to you. So please
say no once in a while!

—J.I., a mother, Florida

Let them play . . . but make sure video games aren't crowding
out other activities when they're with you, like free play, family
conversation, or hobbies.

In other words, don't let your grandchildren substitute virtual
games for real life.

The Santa Controversy . . . or
Did I See You in the Living Room
Last Night, Grandpa?

Let's say you're babysitting for your grandchildren over Christmas.
Enjoy! But you might be faced with one of the big grandparenting dilemmas . . . what to say to your grandchild who asks whether

Santa is real! Do you tell your grandchildren that Santa is not real or hide the facts from them? Do you keep the older grandchildren from spilling the beans to the younger ones? Or do you let them tell the truth?

Pretty simple, you're probably thinking. Let them believe in Santa until they don't. Not so fast, say some. There's actually a Santa controversy going on. Really!

Well, let's look at both sides. . . .

The Anti-Santas

First, there are some child psychologists who say that kids will be so disillusioned when they learn the truth that it's better not to pretend that Santa is real in the first place. They say to tell them the truth from the beginning. . . .

- a schoolteacher in Texas decided to tell her class of six-year-olds the truth recently. It started an uproar among parents and made media headlines.
- a deejay announced that he had a huge "secret" to share with kids. After much prepromotion, he told listeners that it is really *parents* who buy all the gifts—not Santa. It wasn't a popular move!

Also, some clergy are concerned that when kids learn Santa isn't real, they might conclude that God isn't real, either. They feel that younger kids can get confused, and if they start out believing in Santa and eventually learn the truth, their similar belief in God could also be shaken.

Then there are some sociologists who worry that perpetuating the story of Santa keeps the focus on getting presents, and children will miss what Christmas is really all about.

And, finally, many grandparents worry that Santa's handouts may be getting out of hand. (Many foreign businesses agree and suggest that Santa's an American advertisement and marketing tool. In Austria, anti-Santa protesters even denounced Santa as a devilish creation of the Coca-Cola Company.)

The Pro-Santas

Of course, there is some truth to all of the above arguments, but now let's bring back some common sense.

- Children generally discover the truth at about age of seven *on their own* when causal reasoning increases and they see a mismatch with the real world. That is, they understand the high speeds needed to deliver 378 million gifts to 92 million homes in one night. Even Federal Express can't do that!
- Studies find that about two-thirds of children have positive reactions to the truth, not disillusionment, and they're actually proud they figured it out!
- And 50 percent of kids say they still like the idea of Santa even after they learn the truth. They say it helps them enjoy the holidays. (It's the parents who generally say they're sad about their child's discovery!)

The Upshot on Santa

The important thing is, how do the *parents* deal with Santa . . . or the Easter bunny or the tooth fairy or even Big Bird or Barney? Any childhood figure. Follow the lead of the parents. If you "ruin" Santa for the grandkids or if you "perpetuate a silly myth"—depending on how the parents feel—you can guess that the next time you'll be babysitting is when the North Pole freezes over . . . you know what I mean!

That said, there is that tricky age when doubts arise. You may get questions from your grandchildren. Here are a few tips:

1. If you want to know whether your grandchildren are ready for the "truth," ask them what they think is going on. Ask *them* what happens on Christmas Eve, then help them weigh up the evidence.

2. Even when they figure it out, some children still want to believe . . . and that's perfectly okay. *Let them believe.* They won't be damaged or delusional. Santa can be like a comforting imaginary friend.

3. Even with very young children, always add your family values by talking about what Santa represents . . . rewarding good deeds, spreading joy, sharing presents (not just getting them, but also giving and donating).

4. You can also tell your grandchildren the story of Saint Nicholas, the patron saint of children upon whom Father Christmas or Santa Claus is based.

5. And add what different cultures and religions believe. It's a nice way to show your grandchildren that lots of

very different people believe in very similar things, like peace, love, and generosity. It also means they can believe in Santa if they want—or not, and still have the spirit of "Santa."

Happy note: A study at Southeast Missouri State University found that children who'd been read a story about Santa Claus were more likely to share chewing gum with a child in a wheelchair than those who were told stories about the Easter bunny.

Humorous note: Researchers at Mount Sinai School of Medicine published an article in the *Journal of Forensic Sciences* documenting the "Santa Claus syndrome," which afflicts thieves who believe that they can enter a home via the fireplace, and so get stuck in chimneys trying to commit robberies.

Historical note: In 1937, the Salvation Army ordered its bell ringers to stop wearing Santa suits. The group felt that Santas on every corner would only confuse children.

Bottom Line on Babysitting

Having the grandchildren with you—home alone—is not all fun and games, I know. We worry, watch, and wait. We get up in the middle of the night and fade in the middle of the day. We fear the grandchildren won't listen to us and their parents will scold us. We want to teach them, tease them, and mainly touch their hearts. We want them to remember everything we do together that was fun, and remember none of the falls, cuts, or cries.

But even though it's not easy, we do it! And then do it again and again. And love it. Remember the Grandparents.com survey that found 72 percent of us take care of our grandkids on a regular basis, and 81 percent of us have them for part or all of their summer vacation? So when babysitting your grandchildren, keep in mind my tips, be mindful of the parents' wishes, and, most important, use your good sense and obey that loving feeling in your heart.

chapter 9

after the divorce
(not just yours)

Any tough situation seems much worse to us when our children or grandchildren are going through it. We'd like to save them every pain. But we can't. If it's your child who is going through a divorce and your grandchildren are upset, confused, and sad, the best we can do is make things as easy as possible . . . and *not* make it worse!

Grandparents.com asked:

Are you or your grandkids' parents divorced?

The parents are divorced; I'm not.	45%
I'm divorced; the parents are still together.	21%
We're both divorced, and family events are tough.	15%
No, none of us has divorced.	10%
We're both divorced, but everyone gets along.	9%

In a survey of children I conducted for my book *KidStress*, parents' divorce was one of the top stresses for children. This year,

10 million children will go through their parents' divorce. But the ones with grandparents in their lives will have an easier time of it.

- In times of family change or separation, grandparents provide stability to their grandchildren. They maintain routines, drive carpools, and ask about school.
- Grandparents can help the family buffer the financial stresses of divorce by helping to pay for children's school, clothing, camp, or activities—as we discussed in chapter seven, "Grandmoney."
- Grandparents can be there when working parents are not at home or are just feeling overwhelmed.
- Grandparents can give kids more undivided attention than their parents and have more patience than their older brothers or sisters.

The influence of grandparents is so significant that a large-scale survey of adolescents between eleven and sixteen found a strong connection between involved grandparents and teen well-being. In fact, adolescents who had daily contact with at least one grandparent were less likely to use recreational drugs. Why? Most likely it's because grandparents offer conversation, encouragement, and help with solving problems. Grandparents boost kids' self-esteem and help them stay focused on their future.

So your presence in your grandchildren's lives is a saving grace. Another is the fact that, with the divorce rate hovering around 50 percent, your grandchildren will not be alone in dealing with their parents' divorce. Close to half the kids at their school are children of divorce. Reminding them of this may ease their stress just a bit; at least they won't feel like strangers in a strange land. Your grandchildren, your children, and you may also want to talk to some of the parents and their children who have been through divorce already. You'll all see that there is quite often a happy ending.

If your adult child is getting divorced, your grandparenting experience might not be primarily about you and your grandkids flying kites and jumping waves on the beach anymore . . . if it ever was. But that doesn't mean everything has to change. In fact, it shouldn't.

First, try to keep your home, your visits, your babysitting, and the time you spend with your grandchildren as similar as possible to predivorce times. Keep your house a neutral zone for the children, who are very likely caught in the middle of their two parents. When everything else is changing around them, having your home be an island of stability for the grandkids is one of the most comforting things you can do for them.

Next, don't push your grandchildren to tell you their feelings about the divorce. Of course they have feelings about it; they might even think about it all the time. But when they're at Grandma's they get a chance to forget for a while. Remember, you're their grandparent, not their therapist.

On the other hand, if your grandchildren, feeling safe with you, open up and share feelings about their parents' divorce— feelings they are very unlikely to be sharing with their parents— listen, love, and empathize. That won't be hard, because you're likely to be feeling a lot of the same emotions your grandkids are: guilt, anger, sadness, confusion. You're all involved in a difficult situation not of your own making, so you can certainly understand their feelings.

Then, *repeat back* what they say. It's a simple but effective way of letting them know you were really listening, of letting them know that whatever they feel has been accepted by you, and of letting them hear themselves more objectively.

Don't be surprised if your grandchild autocorrects his or her own statements after hearing them repeated by you. For example, this conversation:

> Grandchild: "I'm so angry at my parents for getting a divorce that I'm going to run away."
>
> Grandparent: "Wow. You're so angry that you're going to run away!"
>
> Grandchild: "Well, maybe not run away, but I am very angry."

If your grandchildren open up to you, be positive and reassuring in your responses. Don't tell them that they "shouldn't" say this or that. Don't tell them that their feelings are wrong or right. Just let them know that you hear them, that you are really listening. For example, they may be feeling responsible for the divorce. Instead of telling them that their feeling is wrong, let them know that you understand their feeling, but that the facts are that they are not responsible for the divorce. Although their parents are probably also telling them that is not the case, hearing it from Grandma and Grandpa too is still going to be comforting.

By the way, unless they tell you something that you feel is critical to relay to your adult child—something as serious as physical or emotional danger—it's usually best to keep your grandchildren's confidences. You never want them to feel that you "ratted them out" and that they can't trust you.

The "Ex"

Since many divorces result in the father becoming a noncustodial or part-time parent, often getting visitation every other weekend, it's not surprising that the father's parents often see the grandchildren less frequently postdivorce. That's why it's critical for grandparents to try to maintain a relationship with their son's ex-wife. Even if your adult child is the parent with custody, a positive relationship with your child's ex-spouse can only be good for everyone.

It may be difficult—okay, it probably *will* be difficult—but spend some time with your grandkids *and* the ex if you can. You don't want to be seen as the enemy, because then you'll get shut out. To prevent your adult child from seeing this as a betrayal, have a discussion with them before you do it and explain that you're not being disloyal—you're just trying to protect your relationship with your grandkids. And ask for their suggestions, strategies, and aid. They usually come through for the children's sake.

D-I-V-O-R-C-E

Grandparenting through a divorce is certainly a challenge, but your job is more important than ever. Here are a few ideas to help you deal with your children's D-I-V-O-R-C-E:

D—Don't say nasty things about the ex; it can never help and can only make things worse, alienate you from your grandkids, and put you in the middle of a messy situation. Remember, your child once loved this person—and may still, a little. Saying things like, "She was no good," can be interpreted by your child to mean that you're criticizing them for marrying the "ex" in the first place. And certainly don't say, "He never loved you," or, "She was just after your money," because that sounds like you think that your own child isn't lovable.

I—Involve yourself more than ever in your grandchildren's lives. They need to know your relationship hasn't changed. Give them a safe haven.

V—Venting will be important to both your children and grandchildren. Give them a protected environment to vent. Don't advise; just listen.

O—Offer your love, patience, and support at all times.

R—Respect their space. If your children or grandchildren don't want to talk about the divorce, if they need time to mourn the end of the marriage, give it to them.

C—Comfort your children and grandchildren. Divorce is an enormous loss; it can be as difficult as dealing with a death, and they will need you more than ever.

E—Empathize with your children and grandchildren. Validate all the complicated feelings they are experiencing. The grandchildren especially are likely to experience a jumble of emotions they can't name—and that confusion is also expected and valid and deserving of empathy.

Divorce, whether it's your own, your children's divorce, your parents' divorce, or the divorce of a sibling or good friend, is difficult. Period. And, of course, each situation is different. But there are several universal principles:

1. **Don't trash your child.** Sometimes we inadvertently hurt our child just when they're hurting the most. When you say things like, "You should have shown more interest in his work," or, "You didn't spend enough time with her," you may mean them as constructive advice, but they sound to your child like you're saying the divorce is their fault. What they really need from you is comfort and support so they can get on with parenting your grandchildren and rebuilding their own personal life. If they bring up their own contribution to the downfall of the marriage, you can acknowledge what they say, but don't jump on the blame wagon. They need to hear that no one is perfect and that we all learn from mistakes. They're already injured—don't add insult to injury.

2. **Say less and listen more.** Let your children express their feelings. Don't try to fix things, because you can't. For a parent, it's hard. Even when our children are grown, our parental instincts make us want to protect them from hurtful experiences. But the best we can do is be there, be supportive, and be loving. If you are at a loss about

what to say, try the technique I described before, what psychologist Carl Rogers calls "active listening." Repeat back what your adult child says. Repeat with warmth and sympathy, indicating that you accept the feelings being shared with you. This will reassure them that you have really been listening and give your adult child the chance to hear and consider their own feelings.

3. **Help your adult child help him- or herself.** Taking over for your child will only increase his or her sense of being overwhelmed, helpless, and out of control. Taking over will interfere with any learning that might otherwise result from managing a stress experience. It's natural as parents to want to rush in and fix things. Particularly for our grandchildren's sake. But, since we can't, we certainly should not get in the way of our children fixing them on their own—or at least making the best of them.

4. **Ask for a plan of action.** If your adult child does want to talk, help them to actively manage their situation, to assess the risk-reward ratio of all alternatives. "How do you plan to . . . ?" "What do *you* plan to do?" "Did you ever think that you might also try . . . ?" Let your child suggest steps and come up with ideas. Help them to regain their sense of control and, by doing so, reduce the stress.

5. **Work on their fine-tuning.** That is, help your adult child to focus on the problem without blurring the picture with exaggeration, anxiety, or anticipation. Divorce, particularly when there are children involved, is an

extremely messy, emotional, difficult situation. Help your adult child sort the facts from the fictions. Use phrases like, "From what you're telling me, it seems . . ." "Let me see if I can say that another way. . . ." "What's the most practical way to go about this?" "If you decide to do that, then you'll probably also have to . . ." These will help them navigate their own thoughts.

6. **Provide a safety net.** Discourage withdrawal from friends and family or support systems. In fact, your child should reinforce ties with all those support systems.

Grandparents.com asked:

How did you handle your child's divorce?

I was very supportive, yet fair.	53%
I was supportive, yet one-sided.	37%
I steered clear of the conflict.	5%
I was *not* supportive of the situation.	5%

Encourage them to develop a network of resource people—informal "hotlines." Don't just drop by unannounced or unexpected, but do say things like, "Remember, I'll be around tonight and tomorrow afternoon. . . ." "Let's get together on Saturday. . . ." "Who're you planning to spend the weekend with?"

Grandparents.com asked:

Will you see your grandchildren over the holidays?

Yes, the kids will come to us
and the other grandparents separately.   49%

No, they're spending the holidays
with the other grandparents.   34%

Yes, both sides of the family will
celebrate together.   17%

After the Divorce: Blending

Our adult children want us to be on their side when they're going through the difficulties of divorce. But eventually, we're also supposed to miraculously get along with everyone from all sides of the family on grandchild-centered occasions to which everybody is invited—including new girlfriends, stepparents, ex-spouses, the other grandparents, and the new husband's ex-wife.

It may take years of distance to gain the perspective and compassion to understand that all the players in the drama are struggling as much as we are. *It takes up to four years for newcomers to feel like they're part of a family and for a new family to feel it has a "history."* Until we get there, we must keep in mind that the focus has to be the grandchildren and our relationship with them.

This can be particularly difficult at celebrations like holidays, birthday, graduations, weddings, and other milestone events. Now that the parents are divorced, will there be two birthday parties? Two Thanksgivings? Sometimes yes and sometimes no. Since every family—and every divorce—is different, some families can celebrate together and some can't. If a grandchild's parents' divorce was particularly acrimonious, it may be better to have separate celebrations at first. If things were amicable, joint holidays might work out just fine. Think of the welfare of the grandchildren first, and help your children plan accordingly.

Remember, there's the Brady Bunch family holiday . . . and then there's everybody else's. In my extended family, for example, we've got divorced parents, divorced grandparents, divorced in-laws, stepchildren, half siblings . . . blended Catholic, Protestant, Jewish, and Greek Orthodox religions . . . Italian food, Southern food, and traditional food . . . a grandmother in Boston, a grandfather in California, a grandmother in Florida, a grandfather in Rhode Island, great-grandparents in Ohio. . . . You get the idea!

So deciding where and with whom to celebrate holidays can create a lot of emotional juggling. Some of the problems are logistical, and some of these ideas might work for you.

You could suggest your kids try a "caravan holiday" if many sets of grandparents live near one another—that means they'll take the grandchildren from family to family. If they do, it's helpful to:

1. Put the schedule on paper so you can really see if it works. And make sure your adult children are very realistic. For example, if they're planning to have dinner with you and then dessert with another family, they'll need to plan for

traffic, bad weather, for schedules to be off, and other delays.

2. Tell everyone the plan so no one is hurt. You don't want to get upset if your children suddenly have to get up and leave, and you certainly don't want to be surprised by an unexpected—or uninvited—guest.

3. Preview each stop for the grandkids in the car. Make sure their parents explain new faces, new babies, new stepsiblings, etc. Give them pictures to remind them who everyone is—they may not have seen them for a year!

If your children, and grandchildren, have distant families, and can't be with everyone at the holiday, consider:

1. Make the whole weekend a holiday, rather than just the one day. Easter Sunday becomes Easter weekend. They can visit different grandparents on different days.

2. And grandparents, we need to *stay flexible*! If you get Day Two (the day after Christmas) this year—or the Friday after Thanksgiving—negotiate for Day One next year.

If you have an interfaith or blended family, you'll certainly want to:

1. Find the common message in the holidays. Christmas, Hanukkah, and Kwanzaa all teach us about peace, love, and family. Those are values we all can embrace.

2. Create new rituals of your own. An annual family photo, a traditional menu, or a game you play or story you tell

each year makes any celebration, even if it's not on the actual holiday, a special event.

At every family event, divorce or no, blended family or no, holiday or no, *at every family event* tensions can run high. Here are some dos and don'ts to keep emotions in check in the wake of a divorce:

- **Do be compassionate.** You want to celebrate with your children and grandchildren. You don't want to make them uncomfortable by complaining and competing with other family members.
- **Don't criticize the "other" grandparent.** Reassure your grandkids that they are loved by all family members whether they're at the event or not.
- **Do be flexible.** Even if you don't get to spend the "big" holidays with your grandkids, don't hold a grudge the next time you do see them. Arbor Day can be a wonderful holiday too, if you spend it with people you love.
- **Don't ask kids to choose between you and their other grandparents.** Which grandparents they spend which holiday with is not really up to them anyway, so why add to their burden?
- **Do let them call their "other" parent.** If the grandkids are with you on the holiday, show a little holiday spirit and let them phone or Skype the "ex." The grandchildren will appreciate it—and it won't hurt your relationship with the ex either!
- **Do hang in there!**

During the holidays and all year round when you're dealing with a divorce in the family—especially if it affects your grandchildren—"Hang in there" could be your mantra. But what if that is not enough? What if things have gotten so difficult that you have to actually make them better?

After the Divorce: Mending

Let's say your child's divorce is particularly acrimonious, and perhaps some unfortunate things were said. Let's say you're now estranged from your grandchildren's parents or from the ex who has the custodial rights. Now you don't get to see your grandchildren very much or maybe not at all. When family relationships fall apart, putting them back together is extremely difficult. But it's not impossible. To start on the road to reconciliation, try these steps taken by grandparents who have been there and done that:

1. **Identify the payoff.** It's worth it to reconcile if it means you'll get to see your beloved grandchildren. Write that down, post it on your fridge, really internalize this important point.

2. **Express your feelings to someone other than to your child's ex.** If you vent your frustrations and anger at not being able to be as close to your grandchildren as before, or not at all right now, to a close friend, therapist, or other family member, you might be able to let them go when you reach out to the person from whom you're estranged.

3. **Try to see things from their perspective.** As an exercise, try to see why your grandchildren's parent might be keeping the kids from you. Even if you know they're wrong, it might help you find a strategy for changing things.

4. **Pick up the phone.** Call the parent and ask to schedule a time when they can talk for a little while. Don't expect to settle things on the initial call; stay calm; don't raise your voice.

5. **Acknowledge the pain.** The estrangement from your grandchildren is hurting you, but it's also hurting the grandkids. It would be better for everyone if you could heal and move forward.

6. **Say, "I'm sorry. . . ."** Not as an apology, or even an admission of wrongdoing. You might very well not even know what your child's ex thinks you did. But "I'm sorry" are powerful, healing words, and humans are programmed to respond. You're certainly sorry that there's an estrangement. You're certainly sorry that you and your grandchild are now distant. So you can sincerely say that you are sorry that all that has happened and can ask, "How can I help to make this better?" Express your heartfelt desire to come back together as a family.

7. **Listen to them.** Allow the estranged parent to express their feelings. Don't argue or debate them. Don't interrupt them. In fact, when they're finished ask them if there's anything more they'd like to add. Let them vent whatever pent-up feelings caused the estrangement.

8. **Make a plan.** Ask the parent what they need from you to put things back together. Don't cut them off or rush them. Don't dismiss their request out of hand. On the other hand, don't agree to something you can't bring yourself to do. Listen and tell them that you will think about what they say.

9. **Don't have expectations.** You'd like them to take responsibility for their part in the problem; you'd like them to apologize to you, but don't expect to hear it. It may take time for them to get there—they may never get there! But remember the payoff—it's about the grand-kids. Focus on them.

10. **Forgive.** Staying angry only hurts you and you pay for it in stress, sadness, and wasted energy. It won't change anything to hold the anger and hurt. Life is too short to let negative emotions keep us from the ones we love. Try to forgive for your grandchildren's sake. Try to forgive for your own sake. Even if you don't forget.

Especially when your grandkids are going through a difficult time, like the divorce of their parents, your estrangement is the last thing they need. Grandparents play a critical role in the well-being of children, so when they're going through tough times, we need to step up our game. Refocus your energies on them. Be there, be supportive, and be loving.

Remind your grandchildren that even though their parents aren't going to stay together, something wonderful came out of that relationship and it's them. They are a gift. And both of their parents still love them very much. Beyond that, you love them and their other grandparents love them. And their uncles and other family and wonderful friends love them too.

Your Own Divorce

According to a University of Southern California sociology study, half of all American grandchildren today have at least one set of divorced grandparents. *Fifty percent!* That means that your grandchildren may already have a set of divorced grandparents. Or maybe you're the set that's about to get a divorce.

If you and your spouse are splitting up, you'll first have to tell your adult children. Of course, that may be tough, but telling your grandchildren will probably be even more difficult for you. Here are some things to think about. . . .

Consider that they probably already have friends or cousins with divorced grandparents—and as I said, they might have another set of divorced grandparents already. It might not be that much of a shock at all. On the other hand, they may be very surprised to learn that the grandparents they've always thought were a matched pair are in fact two individuals who are going to lead more separate lives from now on.

As much as you might want to let your grandchildren's parents do the hard job of telling the grandchildren about your divorce, it's usually better if you and your estranged spouse are able to do it too—together, if at all possible. This will show them that you are still united in being their grandparents and still united in loving and caring for them.

When you tell them, here are a few do and don't suggestions:

- **Do choose a time and place to talk to your grandchildren** when neither you nor they are rushed, in a hurry to get somewhere, or late for something. Set aside plenty of time to talk, and do it in a private, quiet, safe, and beloved space.

- **Don't make light of the situation or pretend that nothing will change.** Don't lie—children can see right through that, and they feel it when you're not being honest with them. There will be changes in their lives, but they will not be insurmountable.

- **Do have your grandchildren's parents nearby** or in the room with you to help answer any questions that might arise and to comfort the grandchildren if necessary. Having the parents nearby will also reinforce the idea that the family is still a family, no matter what.

- **Don't go into details you're not comfortable discussing.** Be as honest as you can, but protect your own emotional space.

- **Do be prepared to be unprepared.** Your grandchildren could ask questions that throw you for a loop. "I hadn't thought about that" is a perfectly honest response. Questions could very well come up about possible new relationships, new living arrangements, moving away. And other questions that you just haven't considered at all.

- **Don't be negative, if you can help it.** Even if you're furious and hurt, don't say bad things about your ex or soon-to-be-ex. They are still in your children's and grandchildren's lives and—like it or not—through them, your life too. You can feel all your feelings, but a conversation with your grandchildren is not the time and place to express them.

And finally, do keep whatever you say age-appropriate and in terms your grandchildren can understand. "Grandpa and I have decided that we want to live apart." "Grandma and I are going to live in separate houses." Don't forget, "We will both always be your grandparents and we love you." "We're both going to see you and you can call either one of us anytime, just like always."

Reassure your grandchildren that they are not going to lose a grandparent because of the divorce. Grandparenting is a lifetime appointment, like a judge. Acknowledge that you may not be visiting together, but accent the things that will remain unchanged. When you're finished, let your grandchildren know that they can come to you with any concerns or questions whenever they need to.

Going forward, stay out of your ex's relationship with the grandchildren as much as possible. That is not to say that you should avoid your ex entirely. To the contrary. Try to maintain as positive a relationship as you can. Accept invitations to family gatherings, even if your ex is going to be there. I've been parenting with my ex for more than twenty-five years and grandparenting with him for more than ten years. He's a very funny grandparent, and a loving one, and I get a kick out of seeing the generations that he and I made possible. He and his wife have welcomed me warmly into their home at Thanksgiving, and I have always been delighted to have him (and his second family) when it's my turn with my husband to make the turkey. When we're in grandparent mode, it's not about us! So although it might be difficult to be around your ex at first, do it for your children. Do it for your grandchildren. How bad can a party be if your grandchildren are there?

After all, your unique connection to your grandchildren will not change. You will still be the supportive and loving presence they've always known. You'll still ice those cupcakes and beat them at cards. You'll still encourage them in everything they do. No matter what, some things don't change. And your ex will still be family. No longer a spouse, but part of the family.

Besides, whether it's you or your adult children going through a divorce, you'll find that we humans are built for family life. As I've said before, in a crisis or after a disaster, it's family that gets us through. Seeing our families reduces isolation and depression just by forcing us to have face-to-face contact with other people. And nurturing, researchers have found, triggers innate biochemical stress antidotes. So don't pull out of the family or put it on hold or stay away to avoid your ex. You'll need family as much as it needs you.

Your New Relationship

Let's say you've gotten over your breakup, and so have your children and your grandchildren. Let's say that, because you are a human being with a heart that has begun to open again, you meet someone new. Enjoy it!

But don't forget to look at it from your grandchildren's point of view. To them, this person with whom you feel closeness might seem like a stranger, even an intruder. And they might have doubts, questions, and fears. So here are some suggestions to deal with them:

- Start by asking your grandchild how he feels about your dating. You may be worrying a lot more than you need to about how much *he* may be worrying about it.

- If he is worried, that doesn't mean you should take a vow of chastity and stay home the rest of your life. You're a grandparent, not a Tibetan monk! You're having this conversation to validate your grandchild's feelings and get information to help you steer him toward being more comfortable with the idea of your new relationship.

- Don't ask your grandchild for dating advice. Besides being inappropriate by putting your grandchild into the uncomfortable role of "confidant," it might also make him feel disloyal to your ex and therefore guilty. And then he'll feel doubly guilty if he doesn't like the person you're getting involved with.

- Keep your private life private—at least for a while. Especially if your grandchildren don't live with you, they may not need to know about your new companion just yet. If you are in a multigenerational household, I'd discourage overnights unless your date has spent time with your kids and grandkids, has made friends with them and earned their trust.

- Once a relationship is on firmer ground, be honest about it, direct, and don't be ashamed. But keep things between you and your grandchildren as much the same as possible. Maintain bedtime and mealtime rituals. Reassure them that their other grandparent is still their grandparent and they don't have to stop loving them; nor do they have to start loving your new companion.

- Offer your grandchildren a dose of relationship reality by suggesting that just because you are spending time with a new friend, there's always the chance this new person will not become a lifelong mate. They might become a lifelong friend instead, or a friend for a while. Try to make it the positive learning experience that meeting someone new can offer.

Reassure your grandchildren that this new relationship will not get in the way of your love for them. And let them know that you still have some mixed feelings. Knowing that they are not the only ones struggling with the transition will be comforting for your grandchildren. But, as with all of life's stressors, your grandchild will take his cues from how well you handle this new phase in your life.

Remind them that everyone in their life is a link in the chain of love. If Dad or Mom is not with them on a holiday, there's still Grandma and Grandpa. And sometimes Grandma and Grandpa aren't there, but they have aunts, uncles, cousins, and other grandparents who love them too. Family is like a chain and that chain will never break; it will always be there to support them, because there are so many links of love.

chapter 10

hidden grandparenting stresses

Being a grandparent is fantastic every minute, right? Not a single part of being a grandparent isn't magical and magnificent, right? Of course not. Being a grandparent is fantastic and magical and magnificent . . . sometimes . . . hopefully often. But sometimes being a grandparent can also be stressful, like when grandparenting makes demands we didn't anticipate, throws us a curve we can't easily catch, or creates a problem we're not sure how to fix. Those are the times we're stressed—and we know it. But what about those times when we don't know it? Sometimes grandparenting stress is not so obvious. Sometimes it's veiled by exciting changes, or masked by bigger events, or building so slowly that it slips in before we know it. In other words, sometimes in the midst of all the excitement of grandparenting, we don't recognize the fact that we are under stress too.

The good news is that once we *know* we are stressed, we can address it, contain it, and counteract it. As someone who has spent two decades as a stress researcher at Mount Sinai School of Medicine in New York City, and as a therapist, I know that to be true. So be on the lookout for what I call the "hidden grandparenting stresses." After all, they can't sneak up on us if we are looking for them, and they can't interfere with the fun of grandparenting if we know how to manage them.

Hidden Grandparenting Stress #1:
Changes in Routine

I had a phone call from a friend recently who said she thought there was something very wrong with her mental health. She said that within the past year all her dreams had come true—her daughter married, moved to the suburbs, became pregnant, and made her a grandmother of a beautiful, healthy baby, while she herself had switched to a different campus at the university where she worked, in order to be closer to her new grandchild—but she was crying at the drop of a hat. Why, she asked me, was she so upset when she was so thrilled about all the changes? I had heard similar stories before.

The answer is that change, any change, even good change like becoming a grandparent, can be stressful because it requires adaptation, and adaptation triggers the brain and body's stress reaction: our heart rate, respiration rate, blood pressure, blood sugar level, and hormone levels all prepare for emergencies— the baby has a fever, the babysitter didn't show up, your daughter or daughter-in-law's car broke down and she has a pediatrician appointment, your son or son-in-law has to travel and they need you to stay over . . . you know the story. If the unexpected emergencies pile up, we can become not only physically exhausted, but mentally exhausted too.

The big life changes are, of course, obviously stressful—an illness, a divorce, a retirement, or an economic setback. It's the small changes in a grandparent's life that are less obviously stressful, but they can make their impact felt just the same: a traffic jam on your way to pick up your granddaughter, a missing doll when she's sleeping over, your grandson's favorite DVD is broken, even running out of milk.

> In addition to being a new grandma and baking a mean brownie,
> I was a top real estate broker—in fact, I was doing such great
> business at my firm that they moved me into a bigger office. The
> entire next week, I couldn't get into work, had trouble falling
> asleep, and lost my appetite. It was too much—setting up a baby
> room at the house, buying a car seat, filling the kitchen with a
> high chair, stroller, and jumping jack, and losing my comfortable
> old office too. I rearranged the new office in exactly the same way
> as the old, smaller one had been arranged and at least I felt one
> thing in my life hadn't changed!
>
> —S.T., Nevada

As grandparents, we know that our grandchildren need routines and crave stability. Well, so do we. Therefore, if every little snafu seems to throw you off, try to maintain your other routines as much as possible.

Keep your daily rhythms synchronized.

Did you know that we can use our bodies' natural rhythms to fight stress? So even if you are up late with the new grandchild—or with the older grandchildren on a sleepover—try to get up at your regular time the next morning so your body clock is set—no matter what time you all went to sleep. New research from Chicago's

St. Luke's Medical Center says a regular wake-up schedule is vital for energy and alertness . . . and grandparents need both! Especially if you're over forty, they say! Sorry!

And Dr. Scott Campbell, who studies biological clocks at the Laboratory of Human Chronobiology at New York Hospital, Weill Cornell Medical Center, suggests we should also forget about sleeping late even on weekends! Again, sorry! It's because our biological clock can adapt at the rate of only one hour a day, so oversleep a total of four hours on the weekend and its four days before you're back on track again . . . and then it's the weekend again. The moral? If you're stressed and tired from the grandchildren, go to bed earlier at night, when they go to bed, instead of sleeping later when they leave.

Also, try to get enough early morning sunlight, since it resets our biological clock. Take the grandchildren out for breakfast instead of lingering at home (even though it's easier). And if that's not possible, you can regulate your system with exercise or structured activity, instead. So, as I said before, play, play, play with those grandchildren—it's great for all of you!

Keep your daily schedules regular.

If there's nothing you can do about the change in routine that you're experiencing because you are needed to help out with the newest grandbaby, or have become the caregiver for the older ones, take over the new routine and make it yours. If you are thrown for a loop and forced to adopt a new routine, try to find its advantages to help you regain a sense of choice and control and save you from wasting energy on resistance.

Hidden Grandparenting Stress #2:
Fear of Failure

Need for achievement is built into all of us. It is an extension of our earliest desires to explore, crawl, walk, and run. Now that we are grandparents, it is an expression of our need to gain some control over our concerns about our family and solve some of their problems. But we may also be experiencing fear of failure, and these two drives could be duking it out within us and causing us stress.

> I really wanted to teach my grandson to fly-fish, and I would picture spending future afternoons together. I am an avid fly fisherman, and I've even won several tournaments. But I started to worry that my grandson might not like fly-fishing as much as I do. Or maybe I wouldn't be a very good instructor and my daughter would get mad at me for not being able to teach my grandson. Or even that we would go out for the first time and not catch anything and my fishing buddies would laugh at me. So instead of taking my grandson fly-fishing, I took him to the movies. Isn't that silly?
>
> —P.T., Minnesota

We all have some fear of failure, of course, but when it makes us look at ourselves through other people's eyes instead of looking at the world through our own eyes, it causes grandparents stress! It stops us from trying new things with our grandchildren because we don't want to look silly, and usually leads us to do things the hard way so we have an *excuse* in case we fail. If you catch yourself looking at yourself this way, or procrastinating every time you are about to face a challenge with your grandchild, like taking them on a vacation or trying a new sport, here are some tips:

Have an inside-out perspective.

Look at all situations involving grandparenting through your own eyes only. Don't try to see yourself as others see you—or as you think they see you—from the outside in. We can never really know how others see us anyway. Instead, see the situation from the "inside out"—from your own point of view.

See failure as "inconvenient."

Then, try to experience falling short of a goal as unfortunate, or as a learning experience, or as inconvenient, but not as a failure. And teach your grandchildren the same lesson. *Let them see you fail* once in a while when you are trying something new or something they are showing you. And show them that you expect some failure and are not thrown by it. You will make them braver themselves, and save them from a lot of stress of their own!

Avoid self-blame.

Try your best, but don't put yourself on trial. Particularly in front of your grandchildren. Teach them to be their own defense lawyer— not the lawyer for the prosecution. My mother was great at that.

My daughter, Kimberly, remembers my mother calling her by my name, Georgia, when she was upset and calling to her, "Don't run through the parking lot without holding my hand!" When

Kimberly was insulted by being called the wrong name, my mother said, "Sorry—but if I was perfect, I'd be an angel in heaven—and I'd rather be here with you! Forgive me?" Of course, Kim did—and never forgot the lesson. I now say the same thing to my grandsons, and they do *not* expect me to be perfect. It really reduces my stress!

Don't be a compliment junkie.

Be task-oriented rather than praise-oriented. I know, of course, that it's easier said than done! My friends and I agree—we live for compliments from our adult children, in-laws, and grandchildren, particularly if we've cut back on a lot of other activities to spend more time helping out and having fun with the grandchildren. Compliments are not the only reason we cook holiday meals, take grandchildren for the weekend, pay for the grandchildren's clothes or lessons or camp, travel across the country for our grandchildren's birthday parties, or turn our lives upside down whenever their parents ask us to help out, but *not* getting the compliments certainly does raise our stress levels. Admitting it to yourself helps. Getting sympathy from friends who feel the same way helps too. But here's the best way to move on. . . .

Give yourself credit.

That's right. Pat yourself on the back when you do something right. I mean really reach over your shoulder and pat yourself. Or as my grandmother Sadie did, give yourself a kiss on the hand. Not only is it good for you to acknowledge that you did a good thing, but it gives your children and your grandchildren ideas! They'll give you credit more often and they'll learn to give themselves credit. It's a win-win.

Hidden Grandparenting Stress #3: Loss of Control

If you're like most grandparents, you run around with an undoable to-do list. Then you worry that you're adding stress to your life by adding items to your list. You're not. I've studied stress, written books about stress, and I've treated stress, and I'm happy to tell you that everything you put on that list *by choice* is unlikely to do you any long-lasting harm. It's the things that you *can't* choose, or control, the things you *didn't* predict, that can trigger mental exhaustion and physical stress. It's the gridlock you didn't expect when you are racing to see your grandson perform in the kindergarten play, the dash to the doctor next door with your grandchild after a playground fall, the unexpected trip to babysit because your daughter has the flu, or the race to the hospital because your third grandchild is being born five weeks premature. And yet you probably cross nothing off your list of things to do that day.

So here's my best advice—when something comes up that you don't have control over, don't have a choice about, or didn't predict, *cross something you do have control over off your list*!

I was planning to meet some friends for lunch, and scheduled a stop by the house to transfer the laundry before picking my grandchildren up at school. What I wasn't counting on was the twenty-minute wait for a table at the restaurant. When the hostess told my friends and me that a waiter had a flat tire on his way to work, so they were short a server, I almost bolted for the door. But then I thought about my favorite goat cheese salad that they served and I decided . . . the laundry could get done later! I ate . . . and the grandchildren didn't have to wait.

—M.S., Oregon

Since real life inevitably brings situations beyond our control, management of grandparenting stress has to include the ability to give up the struggle for control when that struggle is unrealistic. Try to change only what you can change, and do it before you invest your adrenaline!

Grandparent Overload

Now, suppose you don't think you have grandparenting stress. Your husband, your friends, your grandchildren's parents all tell you that you seem stressed, but you think you're just tired . . . or distracted . . . or the same as always. How do you recognize when you really are going on Grandparent Stress Overload? There are thinking or "cognitive" symptoms, physical symptoms, and behavioral symptoms. It is good for grandparents to know them, because they can be seen as early warning signs of stress.

Cognitive Signs

The most subtle but most frequent signs of grandparent overload are what I call "the Four Ds." They are cognitive (thinking) symptoms that may make us fear we are aging fast, but are more likely to be symptoms of a bad case of stress.

The Four Ds:

1. **Disorganization** seems to set in first. You know, your cell phone was just in your hand, you haven't left the room, and now it's gone from the face of the earth. And even more worrisome is that when you call it or find it on the high-chair table, you discover that it was right in front of you. But don't worry. It is not your sanity that is in jeopardy; you're just on grandparent overload.

2. **Decision-making difficulties** become obvious next. The big decisions, those of a presidential magnitude, involving Mideast economic policy, are no problem, but what to buy for the grandchildren's lunch when they visit tomorrow can become a major obsession. If it's three o'clock and you haven't decided yet whether to have turkey or tuna, consider that you may be on grandparent overload.

3. **Dependency fantasies** begin to emerge next if the stress is chronic. This means we begin to dream about situations in which we can legitimately be cared for (instead of taking care of everyone else). My grandmother Ida once told me that she dreamed of a week in the hospital for nothing very serious—just a chance to rest, receive flowers, watch TV, be missed by the grandchildren, and be very, very appreciated by the children. That's a dependency fantasy! That's a stressed grandmother!

4. Depression is the final stress symptom in this group. Not necessarily a clinical depression in which you can't sleep or eat, but the "blues"—when all we really want to do is sleep and eat. A trip to the playground seems like a huge deal, and even a trip to get ice cream doesn't tempt you. You are stressed. Read on.

Physical Signs

Next, we have physical symptoms that can hit stressed grandparents too.

- insomnia
- headaches
- allergies (hives, hay fever, and congestion)
- teeth grinding or jaw clenching (temporomandibular joint muscle spasms, or TMJ)
- nausea, indigestion, and heartburn
- backaches and stiff necks
- excessive perspiration

And particularly of note for grandfathers are:

- hypertension (high blood pressure)
- high cholesterol
- chest pain
- peptic ulcer (gastric or duodenal)
- alcoholism
- erectile dysfunction

- premature ejaculation
- failure to ejaculate

Keep in mind that if you're having any of the above symptoms, you should absolutely consult your physician, because you could very well have a medical condition that needs treatment. But if you've been checked out by your doctor and it's not something else, you could very well be suffering from too much stress.

Behavioral Signs

Last, but certainly not least, there are behavioral signs of grandparenting stress. These signs are usually first noticed by your grandchildren! Listen if they tell you that you are acting different, because behavioral signs are observable, repetitive, and usually consistent, and the grandchildren are usually right. They include:

1. **Losing patience.** Are you curt or critical with your spouse, children, or grandchildren?
2. **Withdrawal.** Are you more removed or preoccupied?
3. **Appetite changes.** Are you overeating? I'm not talking about dessert when you go out to dinner. I'm talking about snacking on everything the grandkids and everyone else are eating. Or undereating? Not just skipping a meal here and there, but really losing weight when you don't want to?
4. **Drinking more.** Again, not a celebratory glass of champagne at a retirement party. Are you having that glass of

wine before the grandchildren even leave because you "need it"?

5. **Fatigue.** Are you more tired than you should be, considering your level of activity and the amount of sleep you're getting? Or . . .

6. **Overactivity.** Can you just not sit still at all? Do your grandchildren tell you to stop jiggling your pen or clicking your fingernails on the counter?

Actually, you don't have to add up the number of symptoms you have in order to measure the amount of stress you may be under now. Even having just one or two symptoms probably means that you have grandparenting stress.

"But why now?" my friend Linda asked me. "I got through working, divorcing, and single parenting with fewer stress symptoms than now—and grandparenting is a lot more fun!"

There are a few reasons. First, although we feel young, look young, and act young, we are older than we were as parents—and we're not quite as resilient. Next, as we've said before, we grandparents worry more, not less, when we are with our grandchildren, because our grandchildren are not our children. They are ours to love and enjoy, but we worry that their parents may not be thrilled with our grandparenting or that, God forbid, something may happen to them on our watch. And finally, grandparenting always comes with some changes and unpredictable situations, and as our sense of control goes down, our stress goes up.

But grandparenting stress can be brought down again. It is not a life sentence. It's more like our weight or allergies, just something to be managed. More on this at the end of the chapter, but now, special grandparenting stresses.

Special Grandparenting Stresses

We've talked about the three hidden grandparenting stresses, but there are plenty of additional stresses in all grandparents' lives. They may not even be in our lives directly. Being grandparents, we often feel very acutely the issues and obstacles in the lives of our children and grandchildren. Think of these as as our special grandparenting stresses.

We'll start with how we feel when our grandchildren are stressed.

Grandchild Stress

When your grandchild is stressed, so are you! And sometimes you are the only one seeing their stress. Issues in the lives of our grandchildren can often be overlooked by parents because they're so busy. Also, since you may not see your grandchildren every day, you notice some changes that were gradual and the parents didn't see. According to the Prodigy online survey of over eight hundred children between eight and twelve years old that I designed for *Kid-Stress* (Penguin), these are some of the stresses our grandchildren frequently experience:

- Having to do something unfamiliar.
- Not being allowed to do something they want to do badly.

- Participating in a competition.
- Experiencing body changes, especially when they're out of sync with those of other kids.
- Feeling "little" and perhaps helpless in a world of big people.
- Worrying about conflicts between their parents, or the health of their grandparents.

Remember that not having control is a big source of stress to us grown-ups. Then consider how little control children have over their lives. Someone tells them where they are going to live, where they'll go to school, and who they're going to see during the day. If they're young, someone will likely also tell them when to go to sleep, what to eat, what to wear. It's natural, of course, and children are generally most comfortable in a structured environment. But children who also have some say in their own lives are much more able to deal with stressful events than those who have less self-confidence because they've had fewer choices. So do what you can to help your grandchildren during stress.

- Give your grandchildren options when it's appropriate and support their decisions, whether it's which instrument to study, which friend to call, or which pajamas to leave at your house.
- Give your grandchildren lots of physical and verbal affection when they are under stress. Accept them for who they are, warts and all.
- Encourage (don't push) your grandchildren to try a variety of activities so they can find things they are good at or really enjoy—*their* thing. Let them know it's okay to fail, but let

them try to achieve mastery at their endeavors. As with us, when their sense of control goes up, stress goes down.

• Talk, talk, talk with them. Especially if they seem worried or stressed. Ask questions and then *listen* to their answers. Just getting their worries out in the open is a great stress reliever. After all, everything they worry about when they are alone and awake in the middle of the night seems scarier than when it's said out loud to you in daylight.

• And always, particularly during their times of stress, acknowledge when your grandchildren misbehave but make sure they know that a bad act doesn't make a bad person. This is so important, because there is usually so much more bad behavior when they are stressed, and so much more need for your love and approval at the same time!

Grandbaby Stress

Did you know that infants can have stress too? Under stress, your grandbaby's brain and body prepare for fight or flight, even though they can't do either. Their brain goes on alert and the stress hormone adrenaline activates their startle reflex. They:

• become distracted
• become irritable
• cry more easily
• fuss more often
• lose appetite
• fight sleep
• wake more often during the night

Their body goes on alert too, and muscles become tensed, digestion becomes disrupted, heartbeat increases, blood sugar levels change, and breathing becomes more shallow and rapid. Very short-term stressors, like a dog barking, a fall or tumble, an injection, or a new babysitter are no problem. But long-term baby stress can mean some interference with learning, bonding, and socializing.

The best prescription for older children during times of stress is talk, talk, talk, with us grandparents asking questions and *listening* to their answers. But how do we help deactivate stress in infants, preverbal toddlers, and young children who do not yet have the words to express their stress?

Grandparents can actually encourage a baby's relaxation response by deactivating their own stress response! Here's how it works. Hold your stressed grandchild close and let them feel your tranquillity. When the baby feels your body warmth, hears your slow heartbeat, and is gently rocked by your rhythmic, relaxed breathing, the baby's body will begin to match and mimic yours. Soon your body's relaxation will prime theirs. Their brain will let go of the high-alert mode too, because you will seem so relaxed that they will feel that everything must be fine with the world.

How to breathe like a baby—and why you should learn to do it.

Of course, we can't make our skin feel warm and dry, and our heartbeat slow and steady at will. So how do we create and convey tranquillity when we want to prime our grandchild's calm? We can change our breathing pattern at will, and breathing like a sleeping baby will change your body temperature and your heart rate very quickly. I call it "baby breathing," and it can stop a panic attack or crying jag (or laughing fit) within twenty seconds.

You can learn baby breathing in a few steps.

1. First, picture your grandchild asleep in the car seat. First the belly gently rises, then the belly gently deflates, and then there is a pause. In fact, a sleeping baby's pause lasts long enough to make thousands of grandparents lean over in the car to check the baby!
2. Next, try breathing that way. Gently in, gently out, then pause.
3. Make sure your belly, not your chest, rises and falls.
4. Now close your eyes and count from ten backward to one, taking a breath on each count. Try picturing your breath as your favorite color, so every time you exhale, you're creating more and more of an imaginary mist of that color.
5. Finally, float in that mist until your eyes open.

Baby breathing and the stress response are actually incompatible. We cannot feel calm and crazed at the same time. So breathe like a sleeping baby and your brain will conclude that there's nothing about which to be alarmed. Your grandbaby will come to the same conclusion. Hold her to your chest and practice baby breathing. As you signal the baby that all is well and you are relaxed, your grandbaby will relax as well!

They're Baaa-a-ack: Multigenerational Living

Now, here's a potential stressor—multigenerational living. You love your children and your grandchildren to pieces, but you worry that you might go to pieces if they move back in with you. Well, that's happening quite a bit these days. According to the U.S. Census Bureau Current Population Survey, 6.2 million—or 5.3 percent of all U.S. households—are now multigenerational. And that's up over 20 percent from the previous census report. With rents high, divorce rates high, and the economy in a rut, it's not hard to imagine that the house that was recently so peaceful could soon be full of activity again.

The surprising feedback from grandparents living in multigenerational households is that despite the stresses, there's plenty of upside. From my group on Grandparents.com, I've heard from many grandparents who tell me that not only do they love having their family back under one roof, they also love being needed. It brings purpose to their days and meaning to their lives. The physical demand of keeping up with the grandkids makes them feel younger, outdoor play burns off both calories and tension, and helping with homework provides excellent mental stimulation.

There's a lesson here. We humans are built for family life. In a crisis or after a disaster, it's always family that gets us through. Children must be fed, dressed, and taken to school, so we rally and we do it with a smile. In fact, studies have found that the more we act like everything is okay, the more we actually believe that everything is going to be okay. Family living forces us to have regular, face-to-face contact, which reduces isolation and wards off depression. The predictable routines of family life reduce stress, and the act of nurturing, researchers have found, triggers innate biochemical stress antidotes.

Multigenerational living can have clear benefits for the grandchildren as well. They get to experience what I call the chain of love—learning that more than one adult can care for them. They get to see that if anything should happen to their parents, their grandparents will be there for them. Grandparents can help children get through illness and survive their parents' divorce. Grandparents can help when working couples can't get home for dinner or bedtime, and when single parents are overwhelmed. We can give kids the undivided attention that parents and siblings sometimes can't because of all the demands on their time.

So where are the hidden grandparenting stresses?

- Sometimes it's financial—you watch your bank account dwindle as you try to help your children get on their feet.
- Sometimes it's emotional—you worry that you failed as a parent. Wasn't it your job to raise them to be independent?
- And sometimes it's complicated—you have to deal with so many different agendas, age stages, priorities, and personalities that you are emotionally exhausted.

What can you do if you are feeling less than 100 percent thrilled about your new living situation?

First, know that your feelings are normal, all normal, completely normal. To take away some of the tension, talk with your adult children about your expectations: Perhaps you want to share some expenses, certainly want chores done, and definitely need to make some rules. Make those rules mutually understood. Here's the most important rule:

To live together, you have to agree about what you'll do when you disagree.

Make sure you have some rules about conflict resolution along with house rules about food, housework, and curfews. Some families hold regular meetings, others leave notes, but the bare minimum should be five minutes of direct, face-to-face contact to catch up each day. The more aspects of the situation you feel you've chosen, are in control of, and can predict, the less stressful your new living arrangements will be. And then you can enjoy the extra time with your grandkids!

The Sandwich Generation

Besides the demands of our children and grandchildren, many of us are overwhelmed with the demands of our aging parents. We are catering to the young and the old, caught in the middle like the PB&J in a sandwich—and about to be eaten alive, some of us feel!

It's hard to say whether it is better to have ailing parents nearby or at a distance. If they are close, the constant pressure of doing little things can be exhausting. If they are far away, the constant worry about who is doing the little things you would be doing if you lived closer is exhausting too!

What can you do? Get help! Not psychiatric help for yourself, although you know where to find me, but a team of people to take care of your parents. If they need it, find a nursing service to tend to your parents through their church, community services, Medicaid, local hospital, or city or state aid. If you can, retain a housekeeper to clean and cook meals, or again, find a service through Medicaid. If you are tempted to do it all yourself, go ahead and try it—but know that unless you are a professional nurse/housekeeper/accountant, it's going to be very difficult.

Admitting you need help with these massive responsibilities is not a failure. It is a triumph of recognizing reality. If money is an issue, ask your siblings and even the next generation—your adult children, nieces, and nephews—to help either financially or with time and energy. Nobody can do everything on their own. A situation like this costs too much financially and emotionally. Accepting—that is the first step. Then transform yourself from a servant to a manager. By controlling the situation, you also control the stress.

Grandmother Versus Grandfather Stress

No matter how united a front grandparents may present, they are often different in three significant ways—and those differences can cause grandparenting couples stress.

First, when our grandchildren are experiencing stress or dealing with challenges, grandmothers and grandfathers usually respond quite differently. Of course, each one of us is an individual, so this may not apply to everyone, but as a general rule, grandmothers tend to *empathize* and grandfathers tend to *sympathize*. Here's the difference:

Empathy means that when you care about someone, you don't have to ask or be told that something is wrong. You put yourself in the other person's position. You anticipate what they need from you. You feel what they're feeling. The stress for you is that you can't take over their pain completely, and so for as long as they continue to suffer, so do you. If you can't fix things, you also have the same level of stress as they do—plus the stress of feeling helpless. If the person you are empathizing with feels that you are too involved emotionally, that can cause you even more stress.

Sympathy, on the other hand, means that when you care about someone, you care when they say that something is wrong. You give them advice about what to do to solve their problem. And then you're done. If they bring it up again, you remind them you already told them what to do. The stress for you is that they didn't take or implement your advice. You'd like the situation to be over. You'd like the problem to be solved.

This does not mean that grandmothers are better than grandfathers, or vice versa. Not at all. Although grandparents may argue about which is the better reaction, both empathy and sympathy are valuable, and grandchildren need to experience and learn both. Observe each style with interest and learn from each other. A little of both is probably the best.

Second, Grandpa is not just a deep voice in the nursery. He has a very important role to play in the lives of grandchildren. He is the grandchild's father's or mother's father. Kids love knowing that their parents have someone who can boss them around, scold them, and to whom they have to answer. Especially their Daddy. They want to know they can go to Grandpa and he can sometimes change Daddy's mind. Sometimes it's good that they have an alternative male role model.

Grandma's role is usually seen as helping the grandchildren

value family and remain the latest link in the family chain of love. Grandpa's role, on the other hand, is usually to help children move beyond the family, create their own family, go into the world knowing their family is behind them 100 percent. Grandmothers say "stay"; grandfathers say "go"—and they're both important. Just don't let the differences in your roles, attitudes, or ways of dealing with things become a stressor in your relationship.

Last but not least, grandmothers and grandfathers are often stressed by their differences when it comes to gender issues. For starters, there's the double standard of aging that affects women in a way it does not affect men. Decades ago, Susan Sontag described it this way: "As they grow older, many women keep their age private so that others won't write them off. Most men do not."

This is still somewhat true today. And while we can't change some social stereotypes about grandparents, we can try to change our reaction to them. If you love your laugh lines, that's great. You earned them. But if you don't love them, there are lots of great cosmetics and professional procedures. If you want one, you don't need anyone's permission. But if you feel like you do need permission, you have mine!

Most important, hold on to your youthful feelings. You know you don't feel your age, even though you now have grandchildren. No one does. I still feel about thirty-eight years old inside, and I remember my mother saying in her eighties that when she walked into a room, she always felt like the youngest one there. Revel in the side of you that is still young and the side that is mature. Exercise, eat right, get your checkups, and take care of your health. Parent yourself, pause, and play. Not only will these three Ps help keep the stress at bay, they'll make you feel better and look better.

Now for the Stress Relievers I promised you at the beginning of the chapter.

Stress Relievers

Always remember that *you are entitled to try to reduce the stress in your life.* Just because you are a grandparent does not mean you have to take care of your children and your grandchildren to the detriment of yourself. In fact, take care of yourself at least as well as you take care of your grandchildren—okay, even half as well—and you'll be reducing your stress considerably!

Exercise

When you are exhausted from three grandchildren under the age of five, overwhelmed by your daughter-in-law's hypersensitivity, or completely flooded with adrenaline from calling everyone you know to find the right dentist when your grandson knocked out his front tooth, instead of crawling into bed—because you won't be able to sleep anyway—burn it up! Burn up the stress by dancing around your room. Put on music faster than your heartbeat (about seventy-two beats a minute) to increase your energy and jump around to the beat.

Any sustained, rhythmic, self-regulated physical exercise not only uses up the extra adrenaline that stress stimulates, but it also increases your sense of control, distracts you from your stressors, gives you a sense of accomplishment, and leaves your muscles relaxed. For short-term or emergency stress, try any of these activities to get relief:

- Walking or running
- Swimming
- Tennis or golf
- Biking
- Belly dancing, tap dancing, any dancing!
- Mowing the lawn
- Washing the car

Games

If your physician says no to physical exercise, try games as your short-term intervention. You play them anyway with your grandchildren.

But not just make-believe games or Candy Land. Did you know that competitive games, like cards, backgammon, Wii races, app games, and sports games can also counteract bad stress? They distract you and absorb you. And if you compete openly with your grandchildren or the whole family (instead of always letting everyone else win), you'll also have the opportunity to give yourself the touchdown sign if you win.

Even individual games like jigsaw and crossword puzzles or Sudoku can help—so do them while the grandchildren nap. If you enjoy them and you find them engrossing, they will work against the stress. Plus, you might get the satisfaction of completing the puzzle or solving the Sudoku, thus increasing your sense of control.

Fast Fixes

When your sense of control goes up, stress goes down. So reorganizing any part of your world can also be short-term, fast-fix stress therapy. The grandchildren left a mess? Straightening up can feel like therapy! In fact, our brain does not distinguish the difference between cleaning up the son-in-law problem and cleaning up the closet. Both make us feel better and reduce stress. So do your chores and do in your stress at the same time. Tackle any of these endeavors:

- Clean out your wallet or go through your kitchen junk drawer
- Arrange your closet
- Prune your roses
- Organize your tax documents or balance your checkbook
- Sort your laundry
- Put your photos in an album or compile your recipes

You get the idea. And if it won't increase your stress, have your grandchildren help you—they love to empty out the kitchen junk drawer and look for treasures.

Catch your breath.

Breathe. Really. How often do you just take a few seconds to catch your breath—literally? I find there are times that I'm so busy with two-year-olds at Nate's birthday party or keeping the older boys from tackling each other that I run out of breath and sound hoarse. Do what I do. Stop, lower your shoulders, take some gentle breaths, breathe all the stress out while you look around and take a mental picture of what you see. Enjoy the moment. It may be the only moment of the party or afternoon that you really remember!

Practice laughing.

It works. Deliberately think of a funny incident or joke, or ask your grandchild to tell you one of theirs. Don't wait for laughter to come to you—make it happen.

And smile on purpose. Even if you don't feel like it, just using those muscles in your face actually signals your brain to release the chemicals that make you happy. So when it comes to smiles, follow the saying "fake it till you make it!" Besides, the more you smile, the more everyone around you will smile—and the more relaxed you'll all be.

The grandparenting stresses in our lives are now part of our lives, and so are their symptoms. We cannot ignore them, must not feel guilty about them, and should not let them overwhelm us. I always turn my palm up and look at what is called my lifeline. It has a beginning, a middle, and an end. It does not go on forever. Life, too, has a beginning, a middle, and an end—and it, too, does not go on forever. From now on, whenever you look at your hand, be reminded that the time to reduce stress is now! The time to take care of yourself is now! The time to enjoy your life is now! That way we can grandparent and really enjoy the full, healthy lives we are meant to live.

chapter 11

your way

I really thought that becoming a grandparent would be one of the easiest things I've ever done—after all, the hard part was the parenting, and now all I had to do was babysit and boast. The problem was that I had no practice at it, so I automatically slipped into the role as I'd seen it before. In my case, that meant I began to grandparent the way my mother and grandmother did—Auntie Mame style. I'd show up with gifts, pose for pictures, give advice, go to the park, and then kiss everyone good-bye. This was grandparenting as it was portrayed in hundreds of movies, TV programs, and novels. But none of these ways of grandparenting was *my* way! When my infant grandson needed emergency surgery, I found my way. My way turned out to be emotionally supporting my daughter and son-in-law while they cared for my grandson. He came through it just fine, and I learned that I didn't have to take over—his parents did a great job on their own. And that's still my role and my way to this day.

My daughter parents her children very differently than I parented her—and so much better that I marvel! Her patience and sense of humor are so much greater than mine that I watch and learn. When she wants to talk about a school problem, some sibling rivalry, or an allowance issue, she asks for my advice, and my way is to check the research as well as my experience and then make suggestions. It took some time to meld our styles, but it works. In other words, grandparenting *our* way also means letting our children parent *their* way. So here's to finding your way too—it's always the best way.

Finding Your Way

Having beloved grandparents as role models certainly makes the first step much easier. There will be so much to keep and less to tweak. And since many of the activities and traditions we share with our grandchildren will be tried and true—being the same special things our grandparents did with us—we'll be building a bridge between the past and the future.

Our family stories and traditions help our grandchildren build character and gain perspective on the hectic and confusing process of growing up. Just think about all the things you probably heard from your grandparents: "If you lie down with dogs, you'll get up with fleas"; "If you can't say something nice, don't say anything at all"; and I remember the one my grandmother used to say: "Everything they say and do is information about them, not you." These words might sound old-fashioned—but in fact they're timeless. The transmission of culture through the generations is important, helping kids connect to unchanging truths in a world where everything is shifting around them all the time. Our grandparents often showed a deep understanding about the things we grandchildren needed to know—and now we're hopefully doing the same.

> ### Grandparents.com asked:
>
> Are you like your own grandparents?
>
> Somewhat. I do different things
> but have the same values.   46%
>
> Yes, they were great role models.   30%
>
> No, I go my own way.   12%
>
> No, I didn't grow up with grandparents. 12%

But even if you've learned a vast amount about grandparenting from your own grandparents, your style, interests, and personality might be very different from theirs. Mine certainly are! That means we could very well be a completely different type of grandparent than our own grandparents were. And that's fine. I've seen that there is no single "right way" to grandparent. Just make sure that you're not on automatic pilot or playing a role written by others. Make sure the way you are grandparenting is the way you want to grandparent. If it's not, change it—to your way.

Which Type Are You?

So what type of grandparent are you? Although there are probably as many different types of grandparents as there are grandparents, Grandparents.com has identified a number of basic archetypes. Which one, or more, sounds familiar?

- **The Enforcer**—You don't care how sweetly those little faces smile up at you; the rules are the rules. Someone has to keep order around here, and you aren't afraid to step up.
  - Gift You're Likely to Give: Emily Post's *The Gift of Good Manners.*
  - Best Thing About Being a Grandparent: You relish the opportunity to help a new generation grow up with a strong sense of right and wrong, and you take pride in your good little citizens.
  - Must-have: Your day planner.
  - Your Ideal Day: You take a gang of grandkids out in public and never have to raise your voice. They act like little ladies and gentlemen, and everyone enjoys the day out together—even you.
- **The Spoiler**—For you, being a grandparent means getting all the fun and sweet parts of parenting with none of the responsibility, arguments, and guilt.
  - Gift You're Likely to Give: Whatever the grandkids want. Sky's the limit.
  - Best Thing About Being a Grandparent: The word *yes.* As a parent, you spent decades saying no and you think that was enough. The pleasure of indulging their little fantasies is indescribable.
  - Must-have: Your American Express card.
  - Your Ideal Day: You drive up to their house pulling a bulky trailer. Inside is the beautiful pony of their dreams.
- **The Executive**—You enjoy being a grandparent, but you have come too far to give up on your career now. Your

schedule is more demanding than ever, but you will make time for those sweet faces—when you can.

- Gift You're Likely to Give: The hot toy your assistant read about on the Internet.
- Best Thing About Being a Grandparent: Unplugging. You spend your whole life being accessible by countless forms of communication. Spending time away from it all with your grandkids is a cherished escape.
- Must-have: Your BlackBerry.
- Your Ideal Day: Together you venture into the wilderness and completely off the grid. You milk as much quality time as you can, but are back in time for the next important meeting.

• **The Globetrotter**—After your retirement, you set off to see every corner of the globe, and grandchildren are not going to change that. Besides, you like the kind of role model that you are to them.

- Gift You're Likely to Give: A handheld GPS device.
- Best Thing About Being a Grandparent: You love inspiring your grandchildren to think big and consider the world around them. You also enjoy regaling them with all your exotic stories.
- Must-have: Your guidebook.
- Your Ideal Day: You head out into a vibrant city to go geocaching with them and their eager young minds. You have the kind of amazing scavenger hunt you dreamed of as a child.

- **The Environmentalist**—Prior generations may have under-estimated their impact on the health of our planet, but not you. You know that responsible living is essential for your grandchildren's generation.
  - Gift You're Likely to Give: A wind-power play set.
  - Best Thing About Being a Grandparent: You love passing on a respect for all Earth's creatures and teaching your grandkids to live in harmony with nature. The tickle fights are fun too.
  - Must-have: Your Envirosax reusable shopping bag.
  - Your Ideal Day: You prepare lunch using food from local, sustainable farming and then work in the family garden together.
- **The Buddy**—You take pride in always being in the know. You can tell a "Gossip Girl" from the Cheetah Girls, you showed your grandsons what happens when you mix Mentos and cola, your text-messaging skills are unrivaled, and they call you by your first name.
  - Gift You're Likely to Give: The latest album from synthpop band MGMT.
  - Best Thing About Being a Grandparent: Your grandkids make sure you never grow out of touch.
  - Must-have: Your iPhone.
  - Your Ideal Day: You walk the neighborhood together, just rapping about life, love, and music. Hours pass unnoticed.

We are all, as I said, people, not archetypes. In real life, we are a mix of so many behaviors and feelings that we can't really be categorized so simply. And there are so many more than those on the list above: **the Pushover, the Cuddler, the Coach**, and **the Counselor**, just to name a few, and I'm sure you can add more.

But the archetypes are fun and help us take a look at ourselves, recognize ourselves, smile at ourselves, compare ourselves to our parents and grandparents, and to make more deliberate and conscious choices about how we want to grandparent. That doesn't mean that we have to make a big deal about "changing our ways"—just make an internal note and follow through. We can lighten up or tighten up—once we realize that is what we want to do. We can try saying no more often if we are "Spoilers," and find that saying no does not make us a meanie. We can try saying yes more often if we are "Enforcers," and find giving in a little doesn't make us wishy-washy.

Besides, all "types" are created equal. Different, but equal. So type doesn't matter, so long as you are loving and supportive. Roll around on the floor with them or read them a story—both work. Get involved in whatever they are passionate about or get them excited about your interests—both are great. Tuck them in and read to them or let them stay up and watch TV with them—both are special. As long as you are teaching your grandchildren about love, life, and happiness by example, your way is the right way—for you . . . and for your grandchildren.

Happiness Training

When I ask grandparents what is the one thing they most want to give their grandchildren—more than anything else, they say,

"Happiness." But how do we do that? We can't buy it for them, because the happiness you can buy is short-lived . . . and needs constant repeating or it goes away. We can't bribe them to feel happy with candy, snacks, and late-night TV, because we're just giving them quick fixes and small comforts . . . and that can't go on and on, either. We can't, in other words, make them happy for more than brief intervals, but we can teach them how to make themselves happy. How do you teach your grandchild about happiness? Start by showing them that you are happy and then by sharing some happiness training with them.

As I've said before, we need to model behavior for our grandchildren. And that applies to attitudes as well. Show them that happiness is possible, achievable, and shareable. Honestly, it's contagious. If you are happy, your happiness is likely to rub off on your grandchildren. So . . .

How do you become "happy"? If you are very lucky, you were born happy. People who are born happy have a brain biochemistry that is set on "optimistic." Their serotonin levels remain constant, their dopamine production hums along, and their cognitive style handles life very well. They naturally see the glass as half-full.

The rest of us, however, can still learn to think happy, make it "our way," and teach our grandchildren to think and feel that way too. Studies find that we can actually train ourselves to choose behaviors that create happiness opportunities, and we can actually make conscious decisions to think happy thoughts. And when we act happy and think happy, studies now find that we *feel* happy too. So start happiness training right now and increase the frequency and intensity of happiness in your life!

1. Laugh every day.

Happiness training starts with laughter. Our young grandchildren laugh about four hundred times a day. We adults laugh an average of only fifteen times a day (Stanford University School of Medicine), but it's vital to your health as well as your mind. Here's why:

Just 100 laughs a day will . . .

- give you an aerobic workout equal to that of a ten-minute session on a rowing machine
- increase painkilling (analgesic) endorphins, which also promote a feeling of well-being
- raise your body temperature half a degree, giving you a warm glow
- increase your pulse rate and blood pressure (Northwestern University), which can sharpen your thinking
- enhance respiration and exercise your diaphragm, since during laughter your breath travels from your mouth at nearly seventy miles per hour (Fordham University)
- relax tension, since you can't worry and laugh at the same time
- improve the functioning of your immune systems (Loma Linda University)
- lower your serum cortisol (the hormone produced by stress)
- strengthen the abdominal muscles if you are belly laughing
- burn calories (though to be honest, we don't yet know exactly how many calories a laugh burns up)

So open those e-mail jokes your grandchildren send; share funny stories; watch some funny movies and sitcoms; and never forget to laugh at yourself.

2. Pick friends who are happy.

Happiness is contagious. So, unfortunately, are doom and gloom. So choose friends who spread happiness. Someone else's happiness is a powerful cue. When a friend talks about a happy moment, we automatically scan our memories for similar happy moments. How much better is that than scanning for painful or depressing moments from your past to sympathize with someone who's always complaining? Much better! And happy friends offer another happiness training benefit: They are great role models. Next time you have a hard time seeing any happiness in your day, look at your day through your friend's eyes, and her happy point of view might become yours too.

3. Play, play, play.

Did you know that there is actually a "happy zone" in your brain, and games can stimulate it? Card games, board games, guessing games, all games work—as long as you enjoy them.

Physical play also lights up the "happy zone" in the brain, so grab a grandchild and go outside and play. And if you like sports, don't just watch; participate, because the fine motor components involved in playing just about any sport increase happiness too. How? Apparently the rhythmic movement gives you a sense of mastery and control, and that increases your level of happiness. But don't think you have to run around a tennis or basketball court to feel happy, because miniature golf, cooking new creations, gardening, and even Ping-Pong work too.

4. Set Goals.

More than 225 studies reviewed in American Psychological Association journals found that happy people set more goals, persist longer in achieving them, and are more confident, energetic, likable, and sociable as a result. The goals can be modest, like losing one pound a month for one year, or personal, like making two new friends, or even very private, like trying to find more interests in common with your daughter-in-law. And, of course, they can be tangible, like learning a new language, or taking drum lessons, or learning to play the guitar in Wii Rock Band. Setting goals is a basic part of happiness training, because when your left frontal lobe is setting a goal, your sense of control over your world increases and so does your perceived happiness. If you want to feel young—and happy—forever, never stop setting new goals.

5. Keep a "Happiness Diary."

Record every "up" moment so they won't slip by! They don't have to be only the big moments; the small happy ones count also, like the first e-mail from your grandchild, the thumbs-up from your yoga teacher, or the thank-you from the mother of four you helped in the grocery store. Happiness diaries work on many levels: They help you realize how many happiness moments are already in your life, you'll be more likely to notice if those moments are drop off or are missing, and you'll be motivated to create more of them.

6. Smile!

A reminder: People who smile, even when they don't feel especially happy, can actually change their brain chemistry to mimic happiness. And there's more: When the brain reacts in its "happy mode," sadness is blocked and we feel happy! In other words, since it's impossible to feel a negative and positive emotion at the exact same time, block the bad feelings by thinking about or creating a good one instead. "Voluntarily producing smiles moves [left frontal] brain activity in the direction of spontaneous happiness," say researchers from the University of Wisconsin in Madison. So try it. I put a smiley face on my mirror to remind me to smile. It works. My grandchildren saw the stickers and asked me about them. I explained. They now put them on their mirrors too.

The Secret of Happiness

Here is the bottom line: For happiness to be a major part of our way, it cannot depend solely on outside circumstances. We must wake up every morning knowing that there is happiness potential inside us, and do what we can to find the opportunities to feel it. It is the lesson I learned from my mother, the lesson my daughter learned from her grandmother.

By now I've told you a lot about my mother. I mentioned in chapter one that she was a ten-, twenty-, thirty-, forty-, and fifty-year survivor of cancers. But here's what I haven't told you: She had a mastectomy in her thirties, hysterectomy in her forties, another mastectomy in her fifties, thyroid cancer in her sixties, and stomach cancer in her seventies. She beat them all! Emotionally and spiritually too. After each surgery, she reclaimed her life. After each surgery, she said she felt like she had been given a new gift of life. After each surgery, she redefined her life—more and more "her way." Do you remember that I said she joined me in graduate school, then also got a doctorate, saw patients, and wrote a book too? Now you know why. Each step followed a surgery. She ultimately saw patients who had mastectomies and helped them find their femininity and identity again. She helped couples who were going through health traumas find strength in each other. She lectured and counseled, and even trained Dr. Ruth. She worked and played golf and exercised and danced and traveled until she passed away six years ago—a heart attack! She always told Kimberly and me that she had lived a charmed life—that she had done everything she wanted to do, and that she had it all.

My mother taught us that you can choose how you see life events. . . . She chose to feel lucky! She taught us that you can do things your way. . . . She chose to live fully! She taught us that happiness is not only the result of a wonderful life; it can also help to create one! And that's what I, as a grandparent, want to teach my grandchildren. Teach your grandchildren happiness also.

And now that we know we can become happier each year, here's more great news—we also get better (in many ways) each year.

10 Ways Grandparents Get Better Every Year!

We not only want to give our grandchildren happiness, we want to give them very active and energetic grandparents. That is "our way." Of course, since most of us will be grandparenting for the next three to four decades, we have to expect some hair loss for the guys, some hot flashes for the women, and glasses for everyone. . . . But there's good news too! Science now says there's a whole list of things that actually get better as we get older . . . actually better! And they all help us to be better grandparents. So here we go . . . things the 77.6 million baby boomer grandparents *don't* have to worry about anymore!

First, let's talk about our bodies. . . .

1. **Migraines**—become less frequent . . . and some of us outgrow them completely . . . so the noise of birthday parties, the Wiggles, or Wii Rock Band won't drive you to a darkened room!

2. **Nearsightedness**—improves, until farsightedness takes over, of course, so we get better at reading the tiny cartoons in the grandchildren's bubble gum.

3. **Pimples**—finally go away, because our skin becomes drier, so we're less worried about eating that pizza and chocolate when we're out with the kids!

4. **Allergies**—become milder. In fact, immunologists quoted in *Longevity* magazine say if you don't have them by now, you're probably never going to have them. So go play outside. The grandchildren will never remember the laundry you do for them, but they'll never forget the time you went down the slide with them.

5. **Teeth**—become less sensitive because the nerves and blood supply shrink a little, so you can set a good example when it's time for a dental visit, and . . .

6. **Scarring**—diminishes too, for the same reason (the nerves and blood supply shrink a little). Not only can you show a brave face in front of the grandchildren—you can also go get that plastic surgery if you really want it!

Now, since I'm a psychiatry professor, let's talk about our minds too. There's more good news for baby boomer grandparents:

7. **If you're a type-A personality**—that means aggressive, assertive, and achievement-oriented, expect to mellow out about now, because there's less and less adrenaline for chronic anger. That means more patience for your grandchildren than you had for your children, and maybe more time too, since you're probably somewhat less driven at work now. Guess that's why grandparents are so lovable!

8. **If you're married**—expect to get happier, because, in general, marital happiness increases with every year if you make it through the first twenty-five—making your home a terrific environment for grandchildren!

9. **If you've always been passive**—expect to become more assertive, especially, studies say, with doctors, nurses, school principals, and teachers. Could it be because they are now all younger than you?

10. **If you are mentally healthy**—and you've never suffered from bipolar disorder or psychosis, you probably never will—not even if the grandchildren, or their parents, try to drive you crazy!

Grandparents.com asked:

Are you getting better all the time?

Yes, the grandkids keep me young.	37%
Absolutely; I've never felt better.	28%
No, the years are catching up with me.	19%

So, boomer grandparents, enjoy—these may be the best years of our life!

Making "Our Way" a Better Way

The grandparents who write to me at Grandparents.com and write to one another in my group, "Dr. GG," at Grandparents.com, share a lot of advice, experience, and observations with one another. Some have already been quoted in this book. Much more is waiting for you when you log on. But if you were to ask me as a grandparent, professor, and therapist which pieces of advice have had the greatest impact on me and on my readers, my answer would be this:

Choose to trust your adult children. We learned to be parents. And so will they. Just the act of having faith in them as good parents will encourage them to *be* good parents. And for us, knowing that they are doing their best to be loving parents to our grandchildren lets us step back from the front lines and enjoy the grandparenting experience.

Choose to be open-minded. Our grandkids' parents may have rules we think are unimportant and may ignore things we think are essential, but sometimes they're right. Or, at least, not wrong. Unless you're witnessing abuse, endangerment, or something equally serious, try to take a "wait and see" attitude. You may see something you like.

Choose to forgive. Forgive yourself, forgive your children, forgive. Everybody involved in your grandkids' lives is just trying to do their best. We *all* make mistakes sometimes. And we all need forgiveness sometimes. Giving forgiveness feels even better than receiving it.

Choose human standards. Your son-in-law, your daughter-in-law, your grandkids . . . none of them is perfect. And neither are we. We can't expect perfection, because we are also very human. That's what makes us interesting. So measure everyone by human standards and expect human behavior. "Nobody's perfect" may be a cliché, but it became a cliché because it's true.

Choose to let go. We are the grandparents. Not the parents. We don't control where the grandchildren live, where they vacation, what they eat, or what time they go to bed. We can control only how much this stresses us. Don't let it. Let it go. Let yourself enjoy the time you spend with the grandkids without judgment, without the need to control and fix everything. The serenity prayer commonly used by twelve-step programs applies to grandparenting as well: "God grant me the serenity to accept the things I cannot change, the courage to change the things I can, and the wisdom to know the difference."

Choose love. "And, in the end, the love you take is equal to the love you make," sang the Beatles. Grandparents can be angels of love. We give love, we hope to receive love, and we try to celebrate love. This is the soul of who we are and who we must be . . . for our children, for our grandchildren, and for ourselves.

appendix A

famous grandparents

Did you know that both Paul McCartney and Ringo Starr are grandparents? In fact, we grandparents are a pretty illustrious crowd. We are . . .

Musical Grandparents

Paul McCartney has five grandsons and one granddaughter by his daughters Mary and Stella, the latter of whom is a famous fashion designer.

Ringo Starr once ranked eighth on the *Grand* magazine list of Top 10 Sexiest Celebrity Grandparents.

Steven Tyler is rocking grandparenthood, judging *American Idol* and doting on grandson Milo, by his daughter, actress and model Liv Tyler.

Donny Osmond loves being a grandpa, telling Larry King, "It's the best!"

Mick Jagger is still tearing it up as the front man for the Rolling Stones, still touring, still recording, also enjoying his four grandkids.

Reba McEntire is one of country music's biggest stars, a TV star . . . and a grandma!

Bob Dylan is folk-rock royalty. And, doing everything to the max, he has *nine* grandkids!

Lionel Richie captured our hearts as leader of the Commodores and with his solo work, but his grandchildren, by reality-TV-star daughter Nicole, have captured his heart.

Naomi Judd is a Grammy winner and mother of country singer Wynonna and actress Ashley Judd. And a grandma!

Hollywood Grandparents

Goldie Hawn was voted hottest grandmother by Parentdish. com. A movie star and producer, Goldie's also a grandmother by both her actor children, daughter Kate Hudson and son Oliver Hudson.

Blythe Danner has her daughter, Oscar winner Gwyneth Paltrow, to thank for her lovely grandchildren.

Ron Howard—that's right, Opie Taylor and Richie Cunningham—is a grandfather.

Susan Lucci plays the most endearing and enduring bad girl on daytime television, and she's a grandmother, having celebrated the birth of one of her grandchildren on her very own sixtieth birthday. Now, that's a great present!

Regis and Joy Philbin almost seem like part of our own families, we welcome them into our homes so often. But when they open their home to family, they do so as grand-parents.

Dustin Hoffman has won numerous awards for his acting, but there's no bigger *re*ward than being a grandfather.

Clint Eastwood is an actor, director, musician, producer, and Oscar winner. And also a grandfather. So I'd guess if he asked himself if he feels lucky, the answer would be, "Yes!"

Bill Cosby is the TV dad almost everyone wishes they had and the bestselling author of many books, including *Father-hood*. So it's no surprise that he's now entered grandfather-hood.

Sophia Loren is one hot mama . . . and one hot grandmama!

Pierce Brosnan, a.k.a. James Bond, is a grandfather.

Sean Connery, another James Bond, is also a grandfather. He was knighted by the queen, so you can call him Sir Sean, but he probably likes the title "Grandpa" better.

Joan Rivers is as funny as she is truthful. She once told an interviewer that she didn't like being a grandmother when her grandson was an infant because "I found him very bor-ing." But now she's into it, telling a Canadian newspaper, "I love children, absolutely love them."

Robert De Niro is one of the leading actors of his generation—maybe any generation. And when his grand-children say, "Grandpa," he doesn't have to ask, "Are you talking to me?"

Robert Redford, creator of the Sundance Film Festival and the Sundance Kid himself . . . has Sundance *Grand*kids!

Jane Fonda is an actress, an activist, a businesswoman . . . and a grandmother.

Jon Voight has so many grandchildren by actress daughter Angelina Jolie, he could easily lose count. I know I have!

Harrison Ford may be known to us from his many acting roles, but he told *USA Today* that his grandchildren "know me as Grandpa first." He was named by *Grand* magazine as the "Sexiest Grandparent Alive."

Tony Danza is a grandfather, so when he's asked *Who's the Boss?* the answer is probably his grandson.

Joan Collins has created a little *Dynasty* of her own—through her beloved grandkids.

Martin Sheen is a famous movie star, a famous TV star, a famous father, and now a famous grandfather.

Carol Burnett is a legend in the television and comedy industries with her brilliant series *The Carol Burnett Show,* running eleven years and winning twenty-two Emmy Awards. But she might think that her greatest achievements are her grandkids.

Sally Field, star of stage and screen, is still walking the boards, recently seen on TV's *Brothers and Sisters.* But the brothers and sisters she loves the most are her grandchildren.

Sidney Poitier is an Oscar winner and starred in some of the most iconic movies of our time, but you may not know that aside from his grandchildren, he *also* has great-grandchildren. Now that's . . . great!

Business Grandparents

Donald Trump is still firing on all cylinders. He had his fifth child just fourteen months before his grandchild Kai was born. Busy man!

Warren Buffett might be known as the "Oracle of Omaha" by investors who admire him for his brilliant business instincts, but he's known as "Grandpa" by some of his biggest fans.

Rupert Murdoch sits atop an international media empire, but the big news is . . . he's a grandfather.

Ted Turner revolutionized the television and news industries by creating CNN, but perhaps the biggest revolution in his life happened when he became a grandparent.

T. Boone Pickens made his fortune in the energy industry, which is a good thing, since nothing requires more energy than keeping up with the grandkids!

Political Grandparents

Mitt Romney, former governor of Massachusetts and presidential candidate, has five sons and daughters-in-law and—so far—sixteen grandchildren!

Jimmy Carter, elected president during the nation's bicentennial year, says of grandparenting, "Because [grandparents] are usually free to love and guide and befriend the young without having to take daily responsibility for them, they can often reach out past pride and fear of failure and close the space between generations."

Nancy Pelosi, America's first woman Speaker of the House, likes her grandchildren to call her Grandma Mimi.

General Colin Powell is former chairman of the Joint Chiefs of Staff and former secretary of state, but his grandchildren make him proudest.

Joe Biden is the vice president of the United States, but his highest achievement may be being a grandfather.

Sarah Palin became a grandmother pretty publicly, and she embraced the situation, declaring that her first grandchild will grow up in a loving family.

Marian Robinson didn't get elected, but she's living in the White House, helping her daughter and son-in-law, Michelle and Barack Obama—President Barack Obama—raise their daughters.

Literary Grandparents

Alex Haley is most famous for his *Roots*, but as a grandfather, he's now got shoots.

Maya Angelou is one of America's great poets, an author, and a civil rights activist, and let's hope her grandchildren don't doodle on her thirty National Book Awards!

Frank McCourt, the Pulitzer Prize–winning author of *Angela's Ashes,* has inspired his own granddaughter—who is a teenage writer herself.

Tom Brokaw, TV newsman and the author of *The Greatest Generation*, is now part of the generation of grandparents.

Sports Grandparents

Brett Favre has played quarterback for the Atlanta Falcons, the Green Bay Packers, the New York Jets, and the Minnesota Vikings, but he'll be a grandfather for the rest of his life.

Peggy Fleming brought elegance to the ice as the queen of figure skating, and now she's bringing elegance to being a grandmother.

Muhammad Ali used to float like a butterfly and sting like a bee, but as a grandfather, he needs to be up on his Hungry Hungry Hippos.

Julius Erving—"Dr. J"—was thought to be able to fly across the basketball court when he would begin his dunk from behind the free throw lane, but now he's making his grandkids fly when he pushes them on the swing.

grandparent quote quiz

See if you know who said each of the following quotations about grandparenting. . . .

1. "What children need most are the essentials that grand-parents provide in abundance. They give unconditional love, kindness, patience, humor, comfort, lessons in life. And, most important, cookies."
   A. George H. W. Bush
   B. Paul Newman
   C. Robert Redford
   D. Rudolph Giuliani

2. "A house needs a grandma in it."
   A. Ralph Waldo Emerson
   B. Robert Louis Stevenson
   C. Louisa May Alcott
   D. Ernest Hemingway

3. "Never have children, only grandchildren."
   A. Helen Gurley Brown
   B. Norman Mailer
   C. Anna Wintour
   D. Gore Vidal

4. "When grandparents enter the door, discipline flies out the window."
   A. Ogden Nash
   B. Oprah Winfrey
   C. Olivia de Havilland
   D. Omar Sharif

5. "My grandmother started walking five miles a day when she was sixty. She's ninety-seven now, and we don't know where the hell she is."
   A. Sarah Silverman
   B. Ellen DeGeneres
   C. Whoopi Goldberg
   D. Rosie O'Donnell

6. "My grandmother is over eighty and still doesn't need glasses. Drinks right out of the bottle."
   A. Henny Youngman
   B. Jack Benny
   C. Robert Klein
   D. Red Skelton

7. "Nobody can do for little children what grandparents do. Grandparents sort of sprinkle stardust over the lives of little children."
   A. Jimmy Carter
   B. Alex Haley
   C. Bill Cosby
   D. Billy Graham

8. "Elephants and grandchildren never forget."
   A. Walter Cronkite
   B. Ted Koppel
   C. Mike Wallace
   D. Andy Rooney

9. "The best babysitters, of course, are the baby's grandparents. You feel completely comfortable entrusting your baby to them for long periods, which is why most grandparents flee to Florida."
   A. Billy Crystal
   B. Dave Barry
   C. Maureen Dowd
   D. David Sedaris

10. "A grandmother pretends she doesn't know who you are on Halloween."
    A. Erma Bombeck
    B. Martha Stewart
    C. Oprah Winfrey
    D. Dolly Parton

Answers: 1-D; 2-C; 3-D; 4-A; 5-B; 6-A; 7-B; 8-D; 9-D; 10-A

a new mother-in-law's toast

This was written by Dr. Larry Reed for his wife, Arlene, when she first became a mother-in law. Larry and Arlene are now the grandparents of two! They welcome you to use this toast.

Never have I been before
Deferred to as "the mother-in-law."
That dreaded vision, always maligned:
Too uninvolved, too much entwined,
Far too familiar, way too remote.
May seem reserved, yet tends to gloat.

It's new for me, not before,
Have I ever been the mother-in-law.

And daughters-in-law are supposed to be

Hard to know, hard to see:

Much too ready to disagree,

Mistake the dew for the sea.

Too protective, too selective,

Much too prone to barbed invective.

But all these problems, I foresee,

Are not in store for you (DIL) and me

For we will rise above it all,

Seek out the best, avoid the fall.

But then, my dear, I hope I'm right.

I was never a mother-in-law before this night!

acknowledgments

All my thanks and appreciation to:

Mark Chait, and his parents, who are new grandparents. Thank you, Mark, for wanting the book and for caring so much about it. You are more than its editor—your guidance, real involvement and enthusiasm makes this your book, too.

Scott Gould, my book agent and friend, and to everyone at RLR Associates—you are the best.

Gary Drevich and everyone at Grandparents.com, for an endless wealth of material and for a Web site where grandparents who care can share.

Sarit Catz, who worked with Grandparents.com to bring you the surveys, polls, and grandparents' own words. There was a massive amount of material, but she always found the most pertinent quotes or illustrative survey. It is no wonder that she's won numerous awards including three Writers Guild of America Awards. She has also television, film, radio and theater credits as a writer/producer, won "Clash of the Comics" three times, and teaches sitcom writing at the People's Improv Theater in New York City and at Columbia University's Graduate School of Filmmaking. I am proud to call her both a contributor to this book and a friend!

Dr. Alan and Arlene Lazare, Dr. Lawrence and Arlene Reed, Dr. Constance Freeman and Ellyn Bank for their thoughts and special material.

Kimberly Hope Pauley, my brilliant, funny, supportive and loving daughter, and the mother of my three fantastic grandsons— you are the best mother I have ever known!

Travis Pauley, fabulous father of my grandchildren, my SIL and my "son."

And, as always, thank you to my darling husband, Mike "Jiddo" Tadross, for being my cheerleader.

index